Coventry

The making of a modern city 1939–73

Coventry

The making of a modern city 1939–73

Jeremy and Caroline Gould

Front cover
Tiled mural (Gordon Cullen, artist, 1958) originally on the ramp of the Lower Precinct showing the Belgrade Theatre; Broadgate House and the Hotel Leofric; projects for flats at Hillfields and Spon End; the point block flats at Tile Hill; and, the old and new cathedrals and churches at Tile Hill and Wood End.
[DP164632]

Inside front cover
Coventry city centre looking south-east, 1937. The spires of the Cathedral and Holy Trinity, centre, and Greyfriars, extreme right. The newly created Corporation Street in the foreground with St John the Baptist's Church, right. Works in progress on Trinity Street and the new Owen Owen store facing Broadgate, centre, leading to the New Hippodrome theatre, left.
[EPW053109]

Frontispiece
Coventry city centre looking south-east, 2012. The cross axes of the Upper and Lower Precincts punctuated with Broadgate, left, Mercia House, right, Hillman House (with the pyramid roof), and the double tower of Coventry Point with Shelton Square beyond. The Belgrade Theatre, lower centre.
[26495_030]

Acknowledgements
Levelling Stone, Upper Precinct (Donald Gibson, city architect, and Trevor Tennant, sculptor, 1946). A symbolic phoenix incised into polished Westmorland stone on a Hopton Wood stone background.
[DP164627]

Published by Historic England, The Engine House, Fire Fly Avenue, Swindon SN2 2EH
www.HistoricEngland.org.uk

Historic England is a Government service championing England's heritage and giving expert, constructive advice, and, the English Heritage Trust is a charity caring for the National Heritage Collection of more than 400 historic properties and their collections.

© Historic England 2016

[The views expressed in this book are those of the authors and not necessarily those of Historic England.]

Images (except as otherwise shown) © Historic England, © Crown Copyright. HE, Reproduced by permission of Historic England

First published 2016

ISBN 978-1-84802-245-4

British Library Cataloguing in Publication data
A CIP catalogue record for this book is available from the British Library.

For more information about images from the Archive, contact Archives Services Team, Historic England, The Engine House, Fire Fly Avenue, Swindon SN2 2EH; telephone (01793) 414600.

Brought to publication by Victoria Trainor, Publishing, Historic England.

Typeset in Georgia Pro Light 9.25/13pt
Edited by Susan Kelleher
Page layout by Hybert Design
Printed in the UK by the Pureprint Group Limited.

Contents

Acknowledgements

Jeremy and Caroline Gould are architects and Jeremy Gould is Emeritus Professor of Architecture at Plymouth University and author of *Plymouth: Vision of a modern city* already available in this series. This book is based on research commissioned by English Heritage from Jeremy & Caroline Gould Architects in 2009 entitled *Coventry Planned: The architecture of the plan for Coventry 1940–1978*.

The authors would like to thank the following who have made valuable contributions to the research: Christine Adams and Damien Kimberley of History Centre, Herbert Art Gallery & Museum; Paul Beney, architect formerly of W S Hatrell & Partners and Coventry City Council; Brian (Bill) Berrett, Michael McLellan and Ray Spaxman, architects formerly of Coventry City Council; George Demidowicz and Chris Pancheri, formerly Conservation Officers of Coventry City Council; Robert Gill of Gosford Books; Daffyd Griffiths, architect formerly of W S Hattrell & Partners; Dr Elain Harwood of Historic England; Revd Fr Nicholas Leggett of St Oswald's Church, Tile Hill; Elizabeth Ludgate of Coventry Cathedral; Harry Noble, formerly City Architect and Planning Officer of Coventry City Council; Martin Roberts, senior curator, Herbert Art Gallery & Museum; Ben Stephens; also Somerset County Library; the British Architectural Library, Royal Institute of British Architects and the Coventry History Centre, Coventry City Council.

The authors would also like to thank Christopher Patrick, Conservation and Archaeology Officer at Coventry City Council, and Michael Taylor, formerly of English Heritage, for his help in the early stages of the book and for writing the first draft of the Preface. The following Historic England staff are also thanked: Peter Boland and Kathryn Morrison for their help and enthusiasm in editing the work; Steven Baker and James O Davies for their photography; Damien Grady for the aerial photographs; Philip Sinton for providing the maps; and Robin Taylor and Victoria Trainor for bringing the book to publication with the help of Susan Kelleher, external copyeditor, and Kirstie Ballard at Hybert Design.

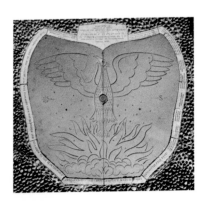

Preface

The planning and architecture of post-war Coventry represents a distinct historic period now lived-through and with known outcomes. The post-war decades are the subject of a growing popular and academic literature and provoke interest among students and researchers – many of them far too young to have 'been there'. This is the result of changing perspectives on the past and an interest in a period when Britain and the world faced the huge challenges of rebuilding the post-war economy and the fabric of ravaged cities, but when there was faith both in the role of the state and public bodies to improve people's lives, and in the ability of ordinary people to influence that change.

Coventry was a leader in the process of post-war renewal and was hugely influential in Britain and abroad. The successive masterplans for the new centre and suburbs informed numerous plans for other cities and the post-war new towns. Coventry also sought to influence the world by embracing the causes of peace and reconciliation, a role adopted particularly by the city's churches and by the new cathedral, and the city set out to be a symbol and a catalyst for a new Europe in the post-war era. The buildings and streets of post-war Coventry are the material evidence of one of the greatest moments in the city's history, a time when Britain and the wider world looked to Coventry for hope and a vision of a better future.

There is no doubt, however, that Coventry has been under-regarded in more recent decades and sometimes poorly treated. If the architectural style of post-war Coventry had been flashier or more ebullient it might have attracted more attention. As it was, the City developed refined and urbane architectural styles drawing influences both from the English Midlands and the wider world, particularly from Scandinavia. Coventry's post-war architecture has been misunderstood and requires time and care to get to know.

This book focuses on the reassessment of the city's important post-war buildings and places. Despite the extensive wartime destruction we can look at Victorian paintings and prints of Coventry and see that many of the most noteworthy buildings from the preceding centuries are still there. The addition of the post-war heritage presents a complex and diverse conservation challenge.

However, this does not mean that the city cannot or should not change to meet the requirements of a different world. Newer developments such as the extension to the Belgrade Theatre, Friargate, the Phoenix Initiative and the pedestrianisation of Broadgate show that there is room for good new ideas amongst a very varied architectural heritage. Historic England encourages its partners – local authorities, community groups, trusts, developers and others – to design change through an understanding and appreciation of the past. If post-war Coventry is significant for the architectural and planning ideas that it embodies and for its social and political context then such significance should be an important consideration in decisions about Coventry's future development. We hope that this book will make a helpful contribution to this process.

1

The city in the 1930s

In the first four decades of the 20th century, Coventry was the fastest growing city in Britain. In 1901 the population of the city was some 70,000 – by 1921 this had increased to 128,000, by 1931 to 167,000 and in 1938 to 230,000, a figure that was immediately raised by the influx of 30,000 munitions workers. The administrative area of the city expanded from 4,147 acres (1,678ha) in 1901 to about 26,000 acres (10,521ha) in 1939. While this expansion took in many of the surrounding villages, the majority of the new population were newcomers from Scotland, Wales and, later, Ireland, drawn by the certainty of work in the ever-expanding engineering industries. Nearly 26,000 new houses were built during the 1930s, the vast majority by private speculators in new suburbs like Radford, Coundon, Stivichall and Cheylesmore. The 19th-century businesses of ribbon making, watchmaking and sewing machines had been replaced by artificial silk, cycles, motor cars, aeroplanes and munitions, and all the components associated with them from machine tools to electrical devices, telephones, magnetos, tyres and engines. The Daimler Company made the first cars in Britain in 1897 at Draper's Field where the Coventry Canal and the mainline railway coincided, and, within a very few years, the famous names of Courtaulds, SS (Jaguar), Triumph, Rover, Alvis, Singer, Armstrong Siddeley, Humber, Hillman and Standard had established factories in the city, many within a short distance of the Cathedral.

The city was dominated by the elegant Gothic spire of St Michael's Cathedral together with the spires of Holy Trinity Church, just to its west, and of Greyfriars in Warwick Lane, which had been incorporated into the new Christchurch between 1830 and 1832. The city retained its medieval plan and silhouette for, although much had been rebuilt in red brick in the 18th and 19th centuries, many of its narrow, cobbled streets and half-timbered houses had survived (Fig 1). J B Priestley in his *English Journey* in 1933 noted that 'you could stage the *Meistersinger* – or film it – in Coventry' and was 'surprised to find how much of the past in soaring stone and carved wood, still remained in the city'.[1] However picturesque it may have appeared, much of the city centre was in poor condition, its housing overcrowded, its factories constricted, its drainage and water supply inadequate and its lanes dangerously congested with ever-increasing traffic. In its scramble for prosperity, Coventry had failed to plan for its industry or its new population and had never attracted the civic benefactors and grand Victorian or Edwardian reordering that had characterised its richer, larger neighbour

Smithford Street photographed in 1939. Deliveries, parked cars and bicycles, through traffic and pedestrians crowded into the busiest shopping street of the old city.
[J Valentine & Sons, ref JV-H-1147; © University of St Andrews Photographic Collection]

Figure 1
Butcher Row looking north photographed c 1880
by Francis Bedford. Furniture is displayed on the
pavement in front of the premises of Palmer & Co,
'Brokers and Furniture Dealers'.
[OP14727]

Birmingham, or the great industrial towns of the north. The new Council House, designed in a Tudor style by Edward Garrett and Henry W Simister of Birmingham for the competition of 1910, seemed rather out of date by the time it was opened in 1920 (Fig 2). There was no large theatre, no permanent museum or art gallery and there was a need for a civic centre containing a police station, courts of justice, public library and further municipal offices. The new Council House enabled Earl Street to be widened with the intention that it be continued into High Street. The plan was immediately thwarted, however, by Barclays Bank (now Yorkshire Bank) who, as early as 1919, refused to move the face of their new building (by Peacock, Bewlay & Cooke of Birmingham) back 7ft (2.13m) to the proposed building line. On the south side, the façades of the National Provincial Bank (1929–30, now NatWest, listed Grade II; Fig 3) by

Figure 2
Council House, Earl Street (Edward Garrett and
Henry W Simister, 1910–20).
[DP172629]

F C R Palmer & W F C Holden, the bank's in-house architects, and Lloyds Bank (1932) by Buckland & Haywood of Birmingham were each set back. Both banks were in a hitherto untried Roman classical style, the National Provincial with a fine Tuscan portico facing down Broadgate. With the wider street, they gave the city centre a new, grand scale.

Figure 3
National Provincial Bank (now NatWest), High Street,
with Broadgate House beyond (F C R Palmer & W F C
Holden, 1929–30).
[DP164619]

The task of replanning fell to Ernest Ford (1884–1955) the city engineer and planning officer appointed in 1924. He had built the southern bypass (the Fletchhampstead and Stonebridge Highways) in the 1930s but without the necessary parliamentary bill, powers (or even budgets) for compulsory purchase or clear policies from his political masters, he was only able to make piecemeal adjustments to the street plan in the city centre when opportunities arose. Plans for a new civic centre and ideas for opening up Broadgate to give views of the Cathedral were only discussed before being abandoned. Ford created Corporation Street (1929–31) from Fleet Street to Chapel Street, around the north-west of the city centre, and Trinity Street (1937), north out of Broadgate. These suggested the beginnings of an inner ring road and radial routes intersecting at Broadgate but they also required the demolition of dozens of houses, including the ancient Butcher Row and Bull Ring. Inevitably, the local press dismissed them 'as patchwork expedients, two isolated, incomplete and separate links'.[2] Nevertheless, the new roads opened up sites for larger shops:

the Co-op rebuilt on West Orchard in 1931 and the new Owen Owen department store, in severe brick with metal windows and a flat roof, opened in 1939 on the west side of Trinity Street, facing into Broadgate. Opposite it, the steel-framed Priory Gate offices (Fig 4) were dressed up in half-timbered 'Tudorbethan' cladding, presumably to match the genuine (and very much smaller) Lych Gate Cottages behind. Trinity Street also served the 2,136-seat

Figure 4
Priory Gate offices (now Wetherspoons), Trinity Street, with Lych Gate Cottages to the right, c 1939.
[DP164620]

Figure 5
New Hippodrome theatre (demolished), Hales Street
(W Stanley Hattrell & Partners, 1936–7).
[J Valentine & Sons, ref JV-G-9578;
© University of St Andrews Photographic Collection]

New Hippodrome theatre (1936–7) by local architects W Stanley Hattrell & Partners, resplendent in its Art Deco curves and jazz-modern decoration, but somewhat incongruous against its diminutive neighbours (Fig 5). It seemed that new architecture in the city could be of any size, scale or style and that none reflected a society concerned with innovation and invention.

The stasis of the ruling Progressive Party (a coalition of Conservatives and Liberals) was overthrown by the municipal election of November 1937 when, for the first time, the Labour Party was returned to power. By gaining control over local education, housing and welfare, power supplies, transport and land, the party believed it could bring about the Socialist society that had been frustrated by the failure of Ramsay MacDonald's Labour Government in 1931.[3] This belief was to shape the planning and architecture of Coventry for the next 30 years. The party was dominated by a triumvirate of councillors – George Hodgkinson, Sidney Stringer and George Halliwell – who served variously as mayors, leaders and on important committees and who dominated the all-powerful, all-party Policy Advisory Committee which recommended capital expenditure and coordinated and prioritised council proposals.[4] Hodgkinson (1893–1986; Fig 6), a trade unionist and permanent secretary to the Coventry Labour Party, in particular was driven by a strong sense of social purpose.

> The Tories and the Liberals had used the functions of local government for minimal change, they were stoppers rather than goers, they had cut our housing proposals by half and were negative in their attitude towards social change. This constituted the challenge for us, and we resolved to quicken the pace and to give a positive and dynamic urge to the work of the local authority.[5]

One of the first acts of the Policy Advisory Committee was to propose the appointment of a city architect and to create a City Architect's Department distinct from Ernest Ford's engineers. Hodgkinson was deliberately seeking someone who was young and not from a conventional local government background, reflecting his administration's desire for change. In January 1939, the 30-year-old Donald Gibson (1908–91) took up his new post.

Figure 6
George Hodgkinson as mayor in 1944.
[Reproduced with permission of the Herbert History Centre Collection; © Culture Coventry]

Gibson and the first plans for the city 1939–41

Figure 7 (below)
Donald Gibson photographed in the 1940s.
[Reproduced with permission of the Herbert History Centre Collection; © Culture Coventry]

Donald Gibson's only experience of local government service was one year as deputy county architect to the rural Isle of Ely (Fig 7). After graduating from the Manchester School of Architecture in 1931, he had worked briefly on materials research at the Building Research Station near Watford and taught construction at the prestigious Liverpool School of Architecture. Here he studied town planning under Professor Patrick Abercrombie (1879–1957), the most important British planner of the period. At the same time (1933–4) Gibson designed his first building – a prototype nursery school at Lache near Chester. With its rational timber frame clad in standard asbestos sheets, this building avoided fashionable styles, reflecting what Walter Gropius, the founder of the Bauhaus, had termed the 'expression of the life of our epoch in clear and crisply simplified forms'.[6] It was a potent precedent for Gibson's architectural programme thereafter. Gibson's new department was 'multi-disciplinary', consisting of staff transferred from the City Engineer's Department, structural engineers, quantity surveyors and, especially, bright, young graduate architects attracted by early responsibility and the unique opportunity. More than 700 graduates applied for 18 new jobs in 1939 for, after the Munich Crisis, private building work had practically ceased and many private offices had closed, awaiting the inevitable outbreak of war.

Prompted by the offer from a local industrialist, Sir Alfred Herbert, to build a new art gallery and by suggestions from the City Guild (the local civic society), Gibson and his 24-year-old assistant and former pupil from Liverpool, Percy Johnson-Marshall (1915–93) immediately began work unofficially on designs for a new civic centre. They sold the ideas to Hodgkinson and the Council by summer 1939 and presented them in May 1940 in a public exhibition entitled 'Coventry of Tomorrow' and subtitled 'Towards a beautiful City' (Fig 8). The project reordered the quarter north and east of the Cathedral and Holy Trinity which was less commercially developed and therefore could be expected to receive general public support. The proposals included 'a new Library, Museum, Civic Hall, Police and Law Courts and Municipal Offices, around a dignified and spacious close … All the buildings were kept comparatively low in order to emphasise the verticality of the Cathedral … and were to be faced with brick and stone to harmonise with the local red sandstone… .'[7] The medieval and 18th-century buildings were cleared away and the neoclassical art gallery (which Gibson was known to dislike) placed on the site already agreed, adjacent to the

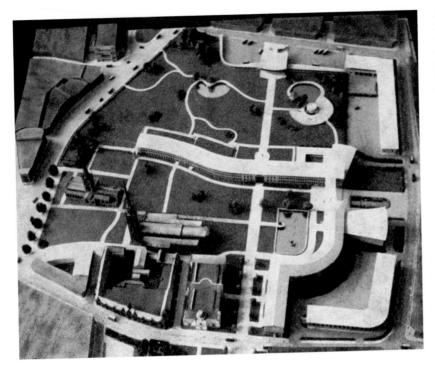

Figure 8
Model of the new civic centre displayed in the 'Coventry of Tomorrow' exhibition (Coventry City Architect's Department, 1939–40). The Cathedral and Holy Trinity are centre left, with Broadgate, extreme left, and the proposed classical Herbert Art Gallery, centre bottom. [Johnson-Marshall 1966, 303, Plate 6; © Edinburgh University Press]

Council House on St Mary Street. The new functions were amalgamated into long, sinuous four-storey blocks set in parkland. The Cathedral was revealed from Broadgate across a green, Holy Trinity was entirely surrounded by lawns while a more informal park with a lake separated the civic centre from a bus station and fire station to the north on Ford Street (now Fairfax Street).

In addition to the civic centre project, 'Coventry of Tomorrow' contained projects from the Architectural Association School of Architecture for an ideal low-density suburb and a Small House Exhibition on loan from the RIBA, presumably intended to suggest how the suburbs of Coventry might be developed. Gibson's aim to 'make the people of Coventry planning and design conscious'[8] was remarkably successful: the exhibition received over 5,000 visitors including nearly all senior school children in the city and the local press wrote enthusiastic reviews. Gibson lectured to schools and other bodies such as the local Rotarians to raise understanding of the planning and design issues.

William Holford (1907–75), Abercrombie's successor as professor of Civic Design at Liverpool, Dr Thomas Sharp, the distinguished town planner from Durham University and the architect Clough Williams-Ellis, gave invited lectures to packed audiences.

'Coventry of Tomorrow' demonstrated Gibson's ability to communicate ideas and his skill at working at a hitherto unthought-of grand scale. Although the somewhat nebulous landscape resembled Le Corbusier's *jardin anglais* in his *The City of Tomorrow* of 1929 (the coincidence of title cannot be accidental), Gibson emphatically rejected Le Corbusier's city of skyscrapers in favour of a more romantic vision of a city still dominated by its old spires. The scale of Gibson's new buildings is akin to Gropius' *zeilenbau* flats[9] (1929) at Siemensstadt, Berlin, which were similarly set in open parkland. Gibson and his staff were also influenced by the writings of Lewis Mumford (1895–1990), the American historian and theorist, so much so that they distributed his *The Culture of Cities* of 1938 to city councillors in an effort to enthuse the Council with new planning ideas. Coventry fitted uncomfortably within Mumford's description of 'the insensate industrial town' and he calls for the 'intelligent absorption' of a plan by the community such that it may be translated into action and adapt itself to changing circumstances. Mumford rejected what he described as monumental, backward-looking, grandiose planning in favour of the 'poly-nucleated city' based on smaller communities surrounding grouped cultural institutions like the civic centre of 'Coventry of Tomorrow', to give 'a social basis of the new urban order'.[10]

The Coventry blitz and development of the 1941 plan

The factories of Coventry were a strategic target for enemy attack. Small air raids started in June 1940 and continued sporadically through the summer but the raid of 14 November 1940 was of a different order. More than five hundred aircraft dropping a mixture of high explosive and incendiary bombs devastated the city centre: only the external walls and spire of the Cathedral were left standing, Jordan Well, Cope Street and Cox Street to its east were badly damaged and in the area west of the Cathedral, the commercial heart of the city, from Trinity Street, Hertford Street and Broadgate across Smithford Street to Corporation Street and Queen Victoria Road barely any structure remained (Fig 9). The half-timbered buildings were especially vulnerable to incendiaries although Ford's Hospital, Bablake School and Bond's Hospital were only partly damaged. Miraculously Holy Trinity Church survived, as did the Council House and St Mary's Hall and the new banks along High Street (*see* p 8). Raids in April 1941 inflicted further damage to the city centre and suburbs and destroyed Christchurch, leaving the isolated steeple of Greyfriars. The raid of 3 August 1942 which damaged Stoke Heath was the last. In all more than 1,000 people were killed and many thousands injured. About 800 shops, over 100 factories and 150 other commercial buildings were destroyed, 23,500 houses destroyed or badly damaged and 53 acres (21ha) of the city centre devastated.

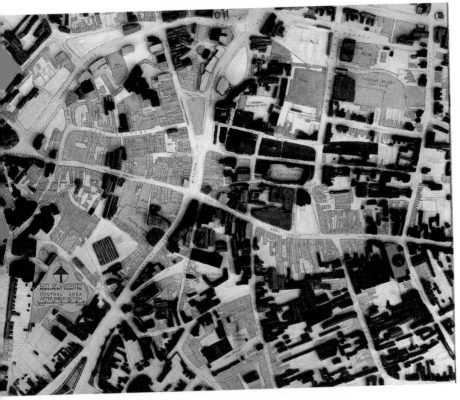

Figure 9
'Central Area after Enemy Action' model (City of Coventry Redevelopment Committee, 1941). Broadgate is in the centre and the cathedral shell centre right.
[© Coventry City Council]

According to Hodgkinson, the 'bombers had done their worst, or in a cruel and cynical way, their best, for the extent of the bombing whilst a tragedy was also an opportunity'.[11] Barely three weeks after the first great raid, when Gibson addressed the Royal Society of Arts in London, he was able not only to lay out how post-war reconstruction generally could be managed (by, for example, using redundant aircraft factories to prefabricate housing components) but also to bring his detailed ideas for comprehensive redevelopment of the city centre to a wider, influential audience. 'In one night the site is largely cleared ready for this regeneration' he stated, 'it rests but with the fortunes of war and the desires of a great people, to see it accomplished.'[12] The City Council too was quick to act. In December 1940 it set up the City Redevelopment Committee and instructed Ford and Gibson to collaborate in preparing a new plan. The Committee was encouraged by Lord Reith, the Minister of Works and Buildings, who advised it in January 1941 to 'plan boldly and comprehensively' and 'not at this stage worry about finance or local boundaries'[13] although this was to become a standard exhortation to other bombed cities and was largely an encouragement to the war effort.

Unsurprisingly, Gibson and Ford could not agree on a single plan and each produced his own. Both were presented in February 1941 to the Development Committee which, by a large majority, endorsed the city architect's plan. Although Ford adapted the 'Coventry of Tomorrow' plan north of the Cathedral and Gibson's idea of an inner circulatory road to the south and east, he retained the existing street pattern and land-use in the central area and what remained of the existing buildings, continuing his pre-war street widening where possible. By contrast, Gibson presented his plan in two stages: the first an 'Intermediate Plan' which improved traffic circulation, opened up access to new sites, retained some existing buildings and started grouping the functional uses – shopping, administration, recreation and business. The second stage 'Ultimate Plan' was much more radical (Fig 10).[14] A circulatory road encircled the whole city centre to connect to the railway station in the south, virtually all the existing buildings within it were removed and the entire road system reconfigured to serve a rectilinear grid of new buildings. These were grouped according to function – the civic centre east of the Cathedral, cultural centre to its south, theatres and cinemas along Corporation Street, shopping and marketplace west of Broadgate, business and commercial adjacent to the railway station and residential east of

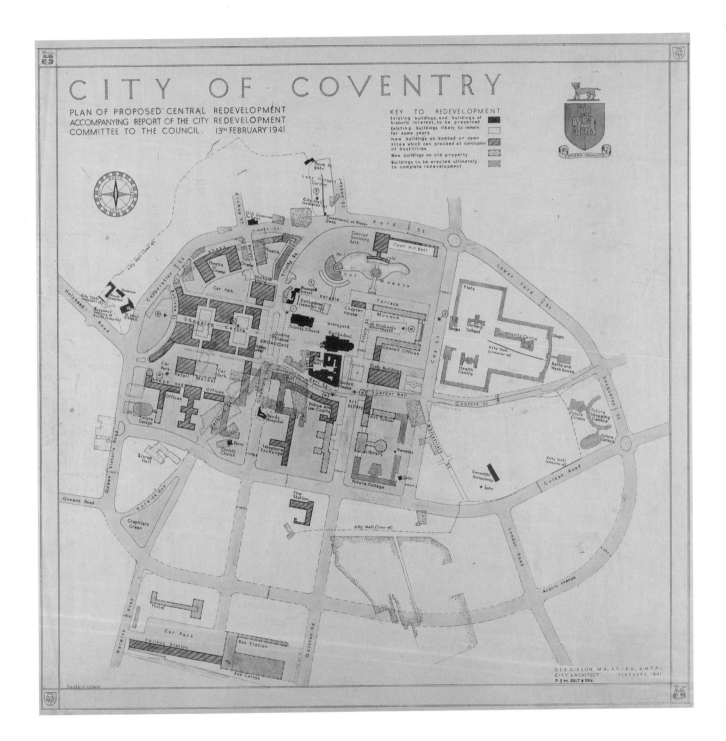

CITY OF COVENTRY

PLAN OF PROPOSED CENTRAL REDEVELOPMENT
ACCOMPANYING REPORT OF THE CITY REDEVELOPMENT
COMMITTEE TO THE COUNCIL. 13TH FEBRUARY 1941

KEY TO REDEVELOPMENT

Existing buildings, and buildings of
historic interest, to be preserved
Existing buildings likely to remain
for some years
New buildings on bombed or open
sites which can proceed at conclusion
of hostilities
New buildings on old property
Buildings to be erected ultimately
to complete redevelopment

CAMERA PRINCIPIS

D. E. E. GIBSON M.A., A.R.I.B.A., A.M.T.P.I.
CITY ARCHITECT   FEBRUARY, 1941
P. J. M. DELT & DES.

Scale 1:2500

Cox Street. A park extended north from the Cathedral Close across Pool Meadow to car parks and a swimming pool on Ford Street, similar to 'Coventry of Tomorrow'. It is in the plan for the shopping centre that Gibson was at his most innovative. This was laid out as two squares on a formal east–west axis centred on the cathedral spire across the reordered Broadgate square and descended the hill to a crescent-shaped open space facing St John's Church on Corporation Street. Broadgate was edged with hotels, a multiple store (to replace the bombed Owen Owen) at the north end, a bridge of offices at the south over Hertford Street and a green running up to the Cathedral and Holy Trinity. The shopping centre was to be arcaded on two levels and pedestrianised, with rear servicing and car parking – the earliest example in Britain of the strict segregation of people and vehicles.

Gibson's 1941 plan set out the principles and the basic form of the city centre redevelopment that was carried through a whole series of iterations to its present form. In its zoning of functions it refers to Le Corbusier, Gropius and to Abercrombie's regional plans published between the wars and their consistent reaction against the muddled functions of the historic city. From Abercrombie's plans, and notably from the *Bristol and Bath Regional Planning Scheme* of 1930, comes the idea of ring roads to direct traffic away from city centres. The grouping of building types into centres or 'precincts' had also been promoted by Abercrombie although the term did not become common until used by H Alker Tripp, assistant commissioner of the Metropolitan Police, in his *Town Planning and Road Traffic* in 1942. A precinct did not have through traffic and was therefore safe from the motor car. The axial, symmetrical geometry of the shopping precinct focussing on the vista of the cathedral spire derives from the Beaux-Arts, the 19th-century French system of architectural planning, which formed the basis of most architectural education in Europe, including at Liverpool under Abercrombie. The form of the shopping precinct was perhaps derived from the great squares of the European city and, according to Johnson-Marshall, the double level referred to the medieval Rows at Chester which he and Gibson knew well. It seems that Gibson was anxious to avoid discussions of architectural style. A series of sketch perspective drawings showed the new buildings mostly in a stripped classical style with columns, arches, pediments and pitched roofs resembling the more conservative town halls of the 1930s. However, in some of the drawings, the buildings take on a markedly Swedish

Figure 10
'Ultimate Plan' for the city centre (Donald Gibson, city architect, 1941). Drawn by Percy Johnson-Marshall. Buildings retained are shown black and new buildings to be built in phases shown red (and cross-hatched), brown and grey.
[Percy Johnson-Marshall collection;
© Edinburgh University]

look, referring perhaps to Ragnar Östberg's Stockholm Town Hall or Ivar Tengbom's Stockholm Concert House (Fig 11). Two beautifully drawn views of the upper precinct and the new Broadgate show a distinctly modern treatment, clearly expressing a regular structural frame with modernist, horizontally proportioned fenestration patterns. They are a clear indication of the direction Gibson would take the final form of the buildings (Fig 12).

By 1941, prompted by the bombing of many other British cities, there was a national surge of interest in town planning and architecture. The Council for the Encouragement of Music and the Arts sponsored a travelling exhibition 'Living in Cities' (1940–1), designed by the architect Ralph Tubbs, which showed how a typical small town could be replanned and also promised 'dignified' surroundings to its cathedral, a city square, city centre parks, a theatre and 'technical institutes, museums and art galleries'.[15] Books like Thomas Sharp's *Town Planning* (1940), J M Richards' *An Introduction to*

Figure 11
'Ultimate Plan' sketch perspective of Civic Buildings from Cox Street (Donald Gibson, city architect, 1941). The Council offices are on the left and the museum on the right, approached through a classical 'Swedish' colonnade.
[Architect & Building News *21 Mar 1941, 194 Viewpoint 3]*

Modern Architecture (1940), the second edition of Abercrombie's *Town and Country Planning* and his *A Plan for Plymouth* (both 1943), the Bournville Trust's *When We Build Again* (1941), the Ministry of Information's *Resurgam* (1943) and the RIBA's exhibition 'Rebuilding Britain' (1943) all told the same story: a new world was around the corner – fresh, clean, bright and modern.

3

Final plans and the building of the Upper Precinct 1941–55

Johnson-Marshall and other key members of Gibson's staff were called up in 1941. The attention of the department turned to building temporary shops, the design of housing estates and, of particular interest to Gibson, the development of experimental prefabricated houses. The development of the 1941 plan proceeded slowly using new female staff – Joan Griffiths and others – and in 1942 the project was given a boost with the gift of £1,000 from Lord Iliffe, owner of the *Midland Daily Telegraph*, to build a model of the entire scheme.

The model, completed in early 1944, was a sophisticated and ambitious resolution of the architecture of the whole city centre (Fig 13). The 1941 shopping precinct became a progression of three squares, separated by large stores projecting forward from the main building lines. A single slab, the Co-operative Society store, terminated the axis at the west end in place of the crescent. At the east end, the axis to Broadgate was marked with twin columns between the shops and an avenue of trees aligned it to the cathedral spire. On the north, three interconnected cinemas/theatres enclosed a radial car park; on the south, the free-standing Market Hall was enclosed by offices, the east range of which were in staggered blocks on the line of Hertford Street. A new triangular park opened to Greyfriars spire. An arc of offices replaced the banks on High Street leading to a formally arranged civic precinct on the line of Little Park Street, facing the old Council House, with a cross-grid of processional ways connecting the various civic buildings. Across Jordan Well, the civic precinct extended northwards behind the Cathedral to the park in Pool Meadow. The new cathedral, designed in 1944 by Sir Giles Gilbert Scott (the designer of Liverpool Anglican Cathedral), had its nave running north–south, connected to the old spire through a cloister formed from the old walls. The redesigned ring road was now dual carriageway at grade with seven roundabout connections; the new buildings, at five to seven storeys high, took on an equally monumental scale. Although the concept remained the same as the 1941 project, the effect of the shopping centre in particular was much bolder, resembling an inter-war Viennese housing *siedlung* or, perhaps more pertinent, the Quarry Hill flats in Leeds, then newly completed.

The 1944 project formed the basis of protracted discussions between the City Council and the newly formed Ministry of Town and Country Planning (MTCP) from whom authorisation was required for the design before compulsory purchase of land and development loans could be given under the

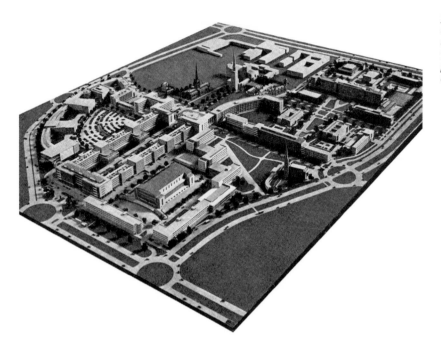

Figure 13
Central Area model from the south-west (Donald
Gibson, city architect, 1944). The Cathedral and Holy
Trinity, centre top, and Greyfriars spire, middle right.
[Johnson-Marshall 1966, 307, Plate 16;
© Edinburgh University Press]

1944 Town and Country Planning Act. The Ministry procrastinated, objecting to the excessive area of the civic precinct (which would produce no rate income), to the arcaded, pedestrianised shopping precinct and to the fact that local interests had not been consulted and that therefore local support for the plan could not be proved. In particular, the Chamber of Commerce and Multiple Shops Federation had stated that without direct vehicular access the shopping area was unworkable. Although the Council was determined to support Gibson's plan unamended, especially in maintaining the area of the civic precinct, by mid-1945 a compromise had been reached with the Chamber of Commerce, partly on the advice of William Holford, now an advisor to the MTCP.

The principal concession was to the shopping precinct where a new trafficked cross street (the future Market Way and Smithford Way) bisected the pedestrian area (Fig 14). The pedestrian route passed beneath it, and parking was allowed along its length, suitably near the shops. The geometry of the shopping precinct reverted to two courtyards, similar to the 1941 plan, and the

Figure 14
'Suggested Plan for Redevelopment of Central Area'
(Donald Gibson, city architect, 1945).
[The Future Coventry, 36; © Coventry City Council]

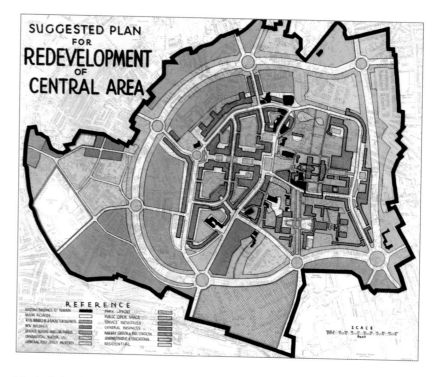

blocks behind the shops to conventional 'doughnut' plans enclosing service yards and car parks. At the west end, the axis opened up to the roundabout opposite St John's Church; the Co-op store migrated north to face Corporation Street and the Market Hall south to face Market Way, both incorporated into perimeter blocks. Hertford Street was reinstated to its original line and the 1944 open space of Greyfriars disappeared to become 'new buildings'[16] and thereby give some additional rateable value. The theatres and cinemas moved to the north side of Corporation Street but, significantly, the civic precinct remained almost as the 1944 model. Most dramatic of all, the ring road vastly expanded. Queen Victoria Road and Corporation Street in the west and Cox Street in the east were left as 'local traffic' roads serving the precincts. A new ring road, still with seven great roundabouts, ran outside them within a band of 'public open space', collecting the radial traffic and encircling the whole city centre. The land within the ring on the west was zoned for 'service industries' (reflecting the current uses); south of the ring for new railway and bus stations; outside the ring on the west, north and east sides for housing. The new central development area was for 452 acres (183ha) – nine times the area of the blitzed city.

The revised hierarchy of ring road and local roads must have come from a detailed reading of Alker Tripp's *Town Planning and Road Traffic*. Road planning and precincts formed the basis of the Ministry's *The Redevelopment of Central Areas* of 1947, a set of standard guidelines for local authorities, although it fell short of recommending pedestrianised precincts for shopping. Otherwise, the guidelines were based on a Coventry-like town and it must have been galling for Gibson for his ideas to be upheld as exemplary but for his plans not to receive immediate approval. But the revised plan of the shopping area lost the liveliness and scale of the 1944 model. The four 'doughnut' courts lack the defining geometry of the pedestrian axis or of Broadgate itself, deriving too exactly from the geometry of the existing streets. The new routes join the old awkwardly. In contrast, the orthogonal geometry of the civic precinct, with its pavilion-like buildings 'laid out rather like a University campus'[17] in a park, seems much more convincing. Gibson's architecture for the shopping area, however, moves assuredly away from classicism, developing from the sketches of 1941. A splendid set-piece perspective of Broadgate by Cyril Farey, the architectural artist, shows a confident composition of regular framed structures with glass infill, flat roofs with heavy cornices and shops recessed under continuous canopies (Fig 15). Gable ends are brick, perhaps like a 1930s block of flats, but the entrance to Hertford Street is a stripped classical arch, set in brick and surrounded by an abstract grid of square-punched windows. As if to remind us of its origins, the main axis is still marked by twin columns, each wittily topped by an elephant borrowed from the city coat of arms. A further sketch perspective shows the overall composition of the shopping precinct: the streets and the corners are marked with larger rectangular blocks, blocks of the same scale enclose Broadgate and lower link blocks connect them. Continuous high-level walkways form canopies to the lower levels, uniting the forms and dividing the axis into separate spaces (Fig 16).

Gibson's revised plan was presented in October 1945 as part of the 'Coventry of the Future' exhibition sponsored by the Association of Architects, Surveyors and Technical Assistants (AASTA)[18] and coinciding with the 600th anniversary of Coventry's Charter of Incorporation and Hodgkinson's year as mayor.

Suggested treatment of the new Broadgate, as viewed from Trinity Church, showing on the left, the entrance to Hertford Street, and in the centre the entrance to Precinct.

Figure 15 (above)
'Suggested treatment of new Broadgate, as viewed from Trinity Church, showing on the left, the entrance to Hertford Street, and in the centre the entrance to Precinct' drawn by Cyril Farey (Donald Gibson, city architect, 1945).
[The Future Coventry, 40; © Coventry City Council]

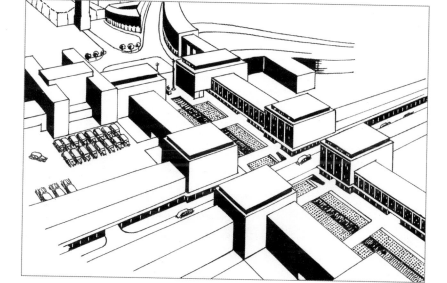

Figure 16 (right)
'An artist's impression of the car parking facilities and service access at rear of Precinct' (Donald Gibson, city architect, 1945).
[The Future Coventry, 37; © Coventry City Council]

The exhibition was opened by Lewis Silkin, the newly appointed Labour Minister of Town and Country Planning. Over 30,000[19] people visited the exhibition and were overwhelmingly supportive; 20,000 copies of the lavish brochure *The Future Coventry* were sold and once again the press, not always well disposed to local Labour politics, was effusive. The Chamber of Commerce supported the revised shopping precinct layout and Labour was returned with an increased majority at the October municipal elections. Here was both the evidence that the City needed in its arguments with Silkin's department and the boost to civic confidence to proceed with the plan. There were no more major revisions and there was a growing impatience to begin construction. A commemorative 'Levelling Stone', designed by Gibson with a symbolic phoenix carved by the sculptor Trevor Tennant (*see* p vi), was placed on the axis of the precinct to celebrate Victory Day in June 1946.[20] Broadgate was laid out in 1947 by the parks director William Shirran – a formal Latin cross of grass planted with trees, shrubs and bulbs donated by the Dutch National Committee (Fig 17). A bronze statue of Lady Godiva (now listed Grade II*) by the sculptor William Reid Dick was donated by William Bassett Green, a local developer. It was planned before 1941 and finally erected in 1949. The City Standard, a 56ft (17m)-high octagonal aluminium mast, topped with a sheet-metal elephant, substituted for the twin columns.[21] The public enquiry was discharged in

Figure 17
Broadgate garden and Godiva statue photographed c 1962 by Eric de Maré showing the landscape of 1947 matured (Donald Gibson, city architect, William Shirran, city parks director, and William Reid Dick, sculptor). In the background Hotel Leofric, left, and Owen Owen (now Primark), right, showing the original glazing patterns.
[AA98/06067]

summer 1946 and the Declaratory Order for the land within the ring road was approved by the MTCP for 274 acres (111ha) in June 1947. The final plan was approved on 16 July 1949. However, by then it was a formality since Coventry's finances had enabled building to start: on 22 May 1948 Princess Elizabeth opened Broadgate square and laid the foundation stone of Broadgate House, the first building of the new city centre.

Broadgate House and the Upper Precinct

Broadgate House (1948–53, now listed Grade II)[22] set the scale and aesthetic for the buildings of Broadgate and the Upper Precinct which were to be built in phases. The intention had been to allow Boots and Burton's to re-establish in Broadgate but they refused to develop mixed-use buildings or to occupy the bridge building over Hertford Street. It was a measure of the confidence in Gibson's plan and of the determination to achieve something more than merely commercial space that the City decided to finance the building itself. Although the basis of the design was set in 1945, Gibson developed it over the next three years with an architectural vocabulary which could be adapted by himself and others for different sizes and shapes of building (Fig 18). The buildings are all on a standard structural grid of 20ft 8in (6.3m) (shopfront) by 23ft 6in (7.2m).

Figure 18
Broadgate House from Broadgate (Donald Gibson, city architect and planning officer, 1948–53).
[DP172621]

The corners and 'solid' parts of Broadgate House are clad in 2½in Blockley City Blend brick perforated with regular 'hole-in-wall' windows edged in white stone and capped with a reconstructed stone cornice. The windows are framed in thin metal casements of a 'square-within-a-square' pattern. A long, projecting window accentuates the upper floor of shops on the flank, north wall. On the lower floors the arcade columns are clad in golden Hornton stone, square on the corners and octagonal elsewhere. On the intermediate façades, the columns and floor slab edges are clad in green Westmorland slate, clearly expressing the structure, and the spandrel panels below the bands of windows are of white travertine. The bridge block is entirely clad in travertine around a grid of square windows, expressing the structural nature of the walls as perforated beams; the fully glazed restaurant is hung underneath. Decorative elements are added in the edge mouldings to the columns, sculptures of 'The People of Coventry' by Trevor Tennant on the south side of the restaurant and in the fanciful clock depicting Lady Godiva and Peeping Tom which overlooks Broadgate (Fig 19). Only in its junction with the National Provincial Bank does Gibson's architecture lose its logical, methodical approach and acknowledge its context; the brick façade curves away under a pitched slate roof, more solid with a set of small windows and then relaxes with a bay of windows copying the classical proportions of its neighbour.

Just as his school at Lache had demonstrated, Gibson was attempting to produce an architecture for his time which rejected questions of style. Architecture would emerge by applying a rational, gridded structure and by codifying structural and functional expression in a limited palette of materials. The architecture would become a framework for controlled change – for example, in the shopfronts or interiors with which he was unconcerned – and a neutral background for human activity. Decoration, especially applied art, could be added in moderation and perhaps he saw this as a means of making the architecture more accessible to the public. The more frivolous decoration of the 1951 Festival of Britain (which he celebrated with a serious exhibition of architectural projects)[23] was studiously avoided. However, he and his team were not immune to outside influences. Brick had always been a part of continental modernism but Gibson was again drawn to Scandinavian examples rather than the more expressionist Dutch or German of Willem Dudok or Erich Mendelsohn. The Swedish welfare state, established by the Social Democratic

Figure 19
Broadgate House and 'Peeping Tom' clock with Lady Godiva on her white horse appearing on the hour (Donald Gibson, city architect and planning officer, and Trevor Tennant, sculptor, 1948–53). The bridge to Hertford Street, right, filled in below the suspended restaurant in 1969; small windows of the link to the National Provincial Bank, left.
[DP164601]

Party after 1932, remained a political as well as architectural exemplar for the fledgling British version and examples of Swedish social housing, schools and community buildings filled the pages of 1940s architectural publications when home-grown examples were in short supply. Their simple forms and defining motifs – repeated square windows, long box windows, plain brick and stone facings, columned arcades and the occasional curved copper roofs – can be seen as the precedents for Gibson's architecture in Coventry.

As both ground landlord and planning authority, the City Council was able to dictate the tenants and developers of the remaining blocks of the Upper Precinct. Although they were all designed by private architects, their form, proportions and materials followed Broadgate House and the models and sketches prepared by Gibson before 1948. The nearest match is the Hotel Leofric (1953–5) by W S Hattrell & Partners on the north side of the axis where the overall form maintains symmetry but the windows and travertine infill to the intermediate block are changed to express the repeat bedrooms of the upper floors (Fig 20). Symmetrical too are the north and south Link Blocks (1954–6), also by Hattrell, which enclose the precinct.[24] Here the patterns of the Broadgate House intermediate block are adapted by setting the glazed façades deep behind

Figure 20
Hotel Leofric, Broadgate. (W S Hattrell & Partners, 1953–5).
[DP164604]

slate-clad structural frames, forming continuous walkways to the upper two floors of offices. The crossing of Market Way and the axis is marked by the near-symmetrical blocks of Marks & Spencer (1953–5, north-east corner) by Norman Jones Sons & Rigby of Southport, British Home Stores (1951–5, south-east) by George Coles of London and Woolworth's (1952–4, south-west, the first part of the Lower Precinct) by Woolworth's staff architect, Harold Winbourne (Figs 21, 22, 23). The blocks break forward of the Link Blocks to form the west entrance to the Upper Precinct, somewhat wider than the gap at the east entrance, exactly as in Gibson's 1945 perspective sketch. The brickwork and the smaller, hole-in-wall windows follow Broadgate House but the innovation is in the grand windows which unite the upper floors. The elevations onto the precincts are all symmetrical: each grand window is of three structural bays – Marks & Spencer divided by Westmorland slate mullions into nine narrow windows, BHS separated into five narrow windows with four brick panel 'mullions' and Woolworth's into three wide windows also with slate mullions. The Market Way elevations are based on similar compositional themes, the most interesting being the corner of BHS which was let to Dolcis shoes (1955) and designed by Ellis Somake, their staff architect. Somake's grand window onto Market Way was an

Figure 21
Marks & Spencer, Upper Precinct/Smithford Way
(Norman Jones Sons & Rigby, 1953–5).
[DP172618]

Figure 22
British Home Stores and Dolcis (now Carphone
Warehouse), Upper Precinct/Market Way (George
Coles, 1951–5). The tall windows which penetrate the
canopy facing Market Way formed the original
shopfront of Dolcis.
[DP172617]

Figure 23
Woolworth's (now Boots), Lower Precinct/Market Way
(Harold Winbourne, Woolworth's staff architect,
1952–4).
[DP172620]

elegant bronze curtain wall of glass and grey Vitrolite panels which, uniquely, ran through slots in the canopy to be continuous with the shopfront. The shopfront columns were clad in figured dark marble which also clad the back wall of the staircase. The interior was an exotic assemblage of contemporary design: the open-tread hardwood stair with bolted glass balustrades, spun aluminium spotlights, tubular steel-framed furniture, abstract patterned carpet and beautifully designed lettering (Fig 24). It was the best of many fine examples of shopfitting (others being the interiors of the Leofric and the Co-op) deliberately designed to contrast with the consistent plain framework that Gibson had devised. The Co-op (1954–6) facing Corporation Street by G S Hay, CWS staff architect, also followed Broadgate House with square windows on the flank wall and a simplified version of the arcade with stone-clad columns (Fig 25). These were decorated with motifs of trades and produced by the sculptor John Skelton who also worked on Broadgate House. The arcading was intended as the prototype for the whole street. Above, the building is a plain brick box (which disguises its awkwardly shaped site) but with the grandest of projecting windows stretching along nine of the eleven bays.

The central square of the Upper Precinct was enclosed by the walkways of the Link Blocks and slim concrete and steel bridges with curved steps at

Figure 24 (above)
Interior of Dolcis, Upper Precinct/Market Way
(Ellis Somake, staff architect to Upsons Ltd, 1955).
[Somake and Hellberg 1956, 83; image acknowledged
to Edgar Hyman]

Figure 25 (left)
Co-operative Store, Corporation Street (G S Hay, CWS
staff architect, 1954–6). Note the original shop sign
lettering on the parapet.
[DP172631]

Figure 26
Upper Precinct landscape photographed c 1962
(Donald Gibson, city architect and planning officer,
1948–55). Walter Ritchie panel below the bridge,
foreground, with the Link Block and Hotel Leofric, left,
Broadgate House, right, and the Cathedral spire,
background right.
[Coventry postcard; © H & L Busst]

either end, all designed by Gibson's office (Fig 26). The splayed walls of the westernmost steps were intended for applied art and the relief panels of 'Man's Struggle' by the sculptor Walter Ritchie were added in 1959 (now relocated to the Herbert Art Gallery).[25] The space was intended for pedestrians to meet and linger: the paving was diagonally patterned brick and concrete slabs, there were interlocking square brick planting boxes, a reflecting pool, wooden benches and flowering cherry trees, all lit by squat mushroom-shaped lamps sprouting from the balustrades. When it was completed in 1955, it was instantly popular and the *Architects' Journal* noted later that it 'was always humming with life, whether in the form of idling in the sun, or political meetings'.[26] The Belfast poet and director of the Herbert Art Gallery, John Hewitt, observed:

> Edged by the double tiers of shops wearing household names, the open piazza, safe for foot-loose children with gossiping mothers: at its zenith on Saturday mornings, with humming swarms of shoppers, time-spenders, chance-met acquaintances, evangelists, folk with perambulators, badged blazers, saris, jeans and, in season, prancing morris-dancers, not a soul abashed by the neighbourly scale of the architecture.[27]

By contrast, Broadgate became a busy roundabout and the main delivery point for buses in the city centre which left its green lawn marooned within the traffic. The north side was completed by the replacement Owen Owen department store (1951–4, now Primark) by Hellberg & Harris of Coventry (Fig 27). This departed from the Broadgate House pattern with a structure of concrete mushroom columns allowing a five-storey glazed curtain wall to face the square. The curtain wall was intensely gridded (now altered and simplified) and framed out in yellow limestone set against a travertine-clad façade. On the ground floor, continuous glazing below the canopy revealed the internal structure and huge, open sales space; on the roof the restaurant was crowned with flattened arches. The composition changed along the east elevation facing Trinity Street to plain horizontal bands of red brick and glazing, anchored at the north-east corner by the stair and lift tower clad in severe black concrete panels. The layers of the composition – panels, glazing and brick – are revealed on the north elevation, the mass of the brickwork emphasised by a grid of tiny porthole windows. The contrast to the plain brick pre-war store could not

have been greater. In its studied asymmetry, composition of cubic forms and accentuated horizontality (particularly in the east elevation), it recalls the pre-war buildings of Mendelsohn in Germany; its roof shape is derived from the Festival of Britain; it develops Gibson's ideas from Broadgate House much further than any other building. Hellberg & Harris gave Coventry one of its very best buildings and one of the few at an appropriate city scale.

Figure 27
Owen Owen (now Primark), Broadgate (Hellberg and Harris, 1952–4). The glazing patterns have been altered, see Fig 17.
[DP164607]

On the retirement of Ernest Ford in 1949, responsibility for planning was incorporated into Gibson's department, giving him the title of city architect and planning officer. For the first time, he was able to integrate the functions of planning and architecture, with multidisciplinary sections responsible for housing (under Gwyn H Morris), schools (William Glare), the city centre (Douglas Beaton) and the overall city development plan (under the planner Wilfred Burns (1923–84)). Gibson and his deputy Fred Pooley (1916–98), at Coventry from 1951 to 1954 and a 'very effective politician',[28] were especially close and shared the burden of committee work and overall strategy. Although the system was ostensibly hierarchical, it was uniquely democratic in its operation, encouraging debate and ideas from all members of the teams whatever their discipline or experience. Such an ethos naturally attracted young, ambitious and left-leaning graduates who had sympathy with the social, economic and political issues that the City was trying to solve. In addition, Gibson energetically supported the aims of AASTA, introduced an architectural model making section and established a technical library, based on the library at the Liverpool School of Architecture and open to all practitioners in the city. Despite the popularity and critical success of his department, buildings like the Upper Precinct and Broadgate House and his personal relationship with Hodgkinson, Gibson constantly battled to get his ideas accepted. He resigned in 1955 after 16 years and one argument too many with his councillors (the exact subject is not recorded). He was immediately appointed chief architect and planner to Nottinghamshire County where his work on prefabricated schools continued to influence Coventry and, finally, he became controller general at the Ministry of Public Building and Works. He was president of the Royal Institute of British Architects from 1964 to 1965 and was knighted in 1962 for services to architecture. Coventry remained his greatest achievement.

4

Ling and the city centre 1955–64

Shops on Market Way with car parking on the roof above (Arthur Ling, city architect and planning officer, 1958–60).
[DP164644]

Figure 28 (below)
Arthur Ling photographed in July 1964 with the model of the halls for Lanchester College and the Cathedral.
[00752626; © Mirrorpix]

By the late 1950s, the austerity of the immediate post-war period had transmuted into unprecedented affluence. The population of Coventry rose from 258,000 in 1951 to 305,000 in 1961, mainly due to the booming motor and engineering industries which employed almost 70 per cent of the local labour force. Although competing for labour with well-paid factory workers, the building industry recovered too and building materials became more plentiful and varied. The new population was young and prosperous. In the period from 1948 to 1960, the number of private cars in Coventry rose from 13,366 to 42,461, an increase of 317 per cent and some 36 per cent above the national average.[29] The demands on the City to provide the infrastructure of the new welfare state – housing, schools, hospitals, clinics and old people's homes – increased, especially as Abercrombie and Jackson's West Midlands Plan, the first approved regional plan in 1951, predicted a population of 360,000 by 1971. Although Gibson's Coventry Development Plan, finally published in 1951, had established planning principles for the city centre and suburbs intended to last 20 years, by 1955 it was clear that these would need substantial revision.

The new city architect and planning officer was Arthur Ling (1913–95) (Fig 28). A graduate of the Bartlett School of Architecture at University College, London, he had worked for the modernist Maxwell Fry (who was in partnership with Walter Gropius) and for Abercrombie and John Forshaw (architect to the London County Council and an Abercrombie pupil from Liverpool) on the County of London Plan, published in 1943. He was a chief planning officer at London County Council from 1945 to 1955 and a senior lecturer in town planning at University College from 1948 to 1955. He was an advocate for Anglo-Soviet cooperation and a communist sympathiser, which, no doubt, endeared him to Hodgkinson and some of his fellow councillors, but he was also a believer in the office organisation of autonomous groups of planners and architects established by Gibson which made the transition easier. The tradition of the Coventry architecture and planning office being a proving ground for young graduates continued but Ling was more interested in principles than detail, and his time at Coventry is marked by the department's output becoming stylistically diverse. Gibson's vocabulary of brick, slate and travertine gave way to new materials such as concrete, precast concrete cladding and lightweight curtain walls. The pace and scale of building accelerated, the first tower blocks of the city arrived, the inner ring road was radically transformed and the City had both the confidence and the means to commence the civic precinct.

Ling and the shopping precincts

Ling's redesign of the shopping precincts continued Gibson's principle of separating pedestrians, private motorcars and servicing. He argued that, once the ring road had been completed, through traffic could be eliminated from Broadgate and it could be 'converted into one immense space' with 'a sense of calm like one experiences in Sienna' (Fig 29). On its east side, he proposed a small piazza between office buildings, a tower to mark the corner of Broadgate and High Street and a route to the Cathedral Close through arcades punched into the classical base of Old County Hall. For Ling, Gibson's proposed axial space was 'out of keeping with the traditional character of Coventry which before the blitz was full of cosy streets' and he was now 'meeting the demand for enclosure of space on a human scale'.[30] Gibson's parking provision in the service courts and along Market Way soon proved inadequate. The bisection of the pedestrian area had always been seen as a compromise and Woolworth's,

Figure 29
Unsigned drawing of the project for Broadgate looking towards the cathedral spire (Arthur Ling, city architect and planning officer, 1958).
[Architectural Design December 1958, 499; reproduced with permission of John Wiley & Sons; © Coventry City Council]

Marks & Spencer and BHS objected to the proposed pedestrian ramps under Market Way because they bypassed their windows. Ling pedestrianised both Market Way and Smithford Way and proposed multi-storey car parks in the service courts at West Orchards, between Market Way and Hertford Street (Barracks) and between the Market and Lower Precinct, the latter being the first open-sided multi-storey car park in Britain. However, he was anxious to preserve the continuity of the shopping streets and not sacrifice land to car parking alone. Hence, he proposed that the roofs of the shops along Market Way and over the Market itself should become car parks, linked with bridges over the pedestrianised streets. He had invented a new architectural form for the motor age which was unique to Coventry.

With the cars eliminated from Market Way, Ling introduced new uses to the precinct to give it a life after the shops were closed. The fourth corner of the crossing became the Locarno dancehall (with Kett & Neve, 1958–60, now the Central Library)[31] and he added two pubs, the City Tavern (1958–60, demolished) next door in Smithford Street, by H Whiteman & Son of Coventry and the free-standing Market Tavern (1956, demolished) by W S Hattrell & Partners, at the south end of Woolworth's. The Locarno was a double-height volume, raised above two levels of shops matching the mass of Woolworth's but only the slate-edged canopy (now demolished) matched the other corners. Above the canopy, the upper shops were faced in white Portland stone; the ballroom in dark-red/grey brick panels separated with blind 'windows' of brightly coloured glass mosaic, designed by the mural artist Fred Millett (Fig 30); the brick was outlined by fascias of white Sicilian marble. Access to the dancehall was by an elegant glass tower and bridge (now demolished), placed in the middle of Smithford Way (Fig 31). This accentuated the entrance, allowed for continuity in the shopping frontage and prevented any attempt to reintroduce traffic to the street. The Locarno was immensely popular. It started out as a venue for ballroom dancing and hosted the BBC's *Come Dancing* and *Miss World* competitions but soon took in popular music. The Thursday night, pay-day dances attracted 2–3,000 people every week and it introduced Coventry's youth to the Rolling Stones, Chuck Berry, Led Zeppelin and Pink Floyd.

The Lower Precinct (1955–60, altered) was developed by the City and intended to attract locally owned shops excluded from the Upper Precinct by

Figure 30 (left)
Locarno dancehall (now City Library), Lower Precinct/ Smithford Way (Arthur Ling, city architect and planning officer, with Kett & Neve and Fred Millett, mural artist, 1958–60). Detail of the façade showing the glass mosaic decoration.
[DP164637]

Figure 31 (below)
Locarno dancehall (now City Library), Smithford Way and (background) Hillman House, Smithford Way (Arthur Ling, city architect and planning officer, with Kett & Neve, 1958–60 and, city architect and planning officer, with Arthur Swift & Partners, 1958–65). The original approach along Smithford Way showing the Locarno dancehall with its glazed stair entrance, the police kiosk and other advertising kiosks.
[Coventry postcard, ref 1-26-03-10; © J Salmon Ltd]

the high rents demanded by the private developers. Ling recognised that the two-level shops of the Upper Precinct had not been completely successful because the stair access was awkward and because some shops occupied both levels with consequent loss of foot traffic. The slope of the site for the Lower Precinct allowed a better arrangement, with a central ramp down to the lower level and two ramps at either side rising to the upper level (Fig 32). The sides of the ramps were decorated with fine tiled murals (1958) by the urbanist and illustrator Gordon Cullen, depicting images of ancient and modern Coventry (now part demolished, part relocated). Although the ground plan was similar to the Upper Precinct, there was no demand for offices and the precinct consisted of two levels of shops with storage above. The bays were framed out in Westmorland slate with shallow pitched roof gables filled with alternating panels of glazing and bright neon panels depicting Coventry industries. The upper level

Figure 32
Lower Precinct and Lady Godiva Café photographed in
1971 (Arthur Ling, city architect and planning officer,
1955–60).
[© Coventry City Council]

shopfronts were set back and the roof projected to give some protection from the weather. The gallery balustrade was of cast aluminium panels, the abstract patterns based on motor crankshafts, rather than the Festival-like zigzag steel of the Upper Precinct.

While the symmetry of the Lower Precinct was retained, Ling's search for a new 'human scale' questioned Gibson's Beaux-Arts axis and his ideas of creating vistas. To this end a central, circular café was added to 'add interest' and a 16-storey block of flats over three storeys of shops, Mercia House, at the west end to give 'an intimate feeling of enclosure' to the precinct.[32] The same principle was applied to Smithford Way: the Locarno stair added the interest and, at the north end junction with Corporation Street, a 13-storey block of flats, Hillman House, sat on top of a three-storey plinth of offices. Mercia House and Hillman House both contained flats for 'professional people without families', the first housing within the city centre and a major departure from Gibson's strict functional zoning. Since they competed with the 'traditional and symbolic skyline' of the three spires, Ling required that the profiles of the towers create an 'interesting skyline'. Hillman House (1958–65),[33] designed in association with Arthur Swift & Partners, added triangular glazed balconies to an otherwise square plan, giving a superficial resemblance to Frank Lloyd Wright's Price Tower at Bartlesville, Oklahoma of 1952–6 (see Fig 31). The roof was terminated with a pyramidal crown and flèche; the plinth, clad in a curtain wall of glass and dark-green mosaic panels, bent incongruously along Corporation Street. By contrast, Ling's Mercia House (1962–7)[34] was a slim tower of white mosaic-tiled horizontal bands perched elegantly on its white plinth (containing the C&A store designed with North & Partners of Maidenhead) which integrated effortlessly with the precinct gallery (Fig 33). Plinth and tower were separated by the full-height glazing of the fourth-floor restaurant, its columned structure just visible behind the glass. The circular Lady Godiva Café (1957–8, altered)[35] was a cylindrical pillbox shape, cantilevering from a structural foot and accessed from the gallery via a bridge. The curved glass windows were divided by black external mullions and retractable blinds projected from the southern perimeter. The sense of theatrical display was especially effective on winter evenings and the *Architects' Journal* reported it as 'thoroughly used by the populace' and recommended the black coffee with cream.[36]

Figure 33
Mercia House, Lower Precinct and C&A store (now shops), below (Arthur Ling, city architect and planning officer, with North & Partners, 1962–7). [DP164634]

Lijnbaan shopping centre, Rotterdam, The Netherlands (Van den Broek & Bakema, 1951–3). Arthur Ling, foreground left, visiting with delegates to the International Union of Architects Congress in June 1955.
[© Bill Berrett]

Market Way followed the route to Queen Victoria Road that Gibson had planned. Now that it was pedestrianised, Ling 'enclosed the space' of the existing straight section by proposing a 16-storey hotel (1962) to balance Hillman House across the axis.[37] With no developers forthcoming, Ling substituted a cross canopy, a device borrowed from the Lijnbaan shopping street in Rotterdam (1951–3) by Van den Broek & Bakema, which had been fêted in the architectural magazines and which was at a similar scale to Market Way (Fig 34). The transition to the curved section was marked by the white tiled cube of the Gas Board's showroom (1964) and the Market Tavern, but thereafter the design relied on the standard 20ft (6.1m) shop module, expressed in deep reconstructed stone frames infilled with simple glazing patterns, and with continuous canopies similar to the Lijnbaan (*see* p 34). The street then linked under a bridge of offices (with the car bridge over, now demolished) to a new square, Shelton Square. The route continued as the City Arcade, turning under a hexagonal glazed roof (originally an aviary), narrowing and widening again before emerging onto Queen Victoria Road. City Arcade (1960–2)[38] was distinguished by the neat bay-windowed shopfronts and the standard projecting signs all designed by Ling's department (Fig 35). Shelton Square[39] acted as a pivot, directing pedestrians to

City Arcade (Arthur Ling, city architect and planning officer, 1960–2).
[Hewitt 1966, 11; © Coventry County Council]

the Arcade, under an office block to (the future) Bull Yard and to Hertford Street and through the shops under the bridge on the east side to the City Market. Ling's plan is picturesque and intricate when compared to Gibson's axial precincts. Though this was pragmatic (there was only a demand for small shops and some offices), Ling's ideas were influenced by Gordon Cullen's 'Townscape', a series of important articles published through the 1950s in the *Architectural Review*. Cullen analysed the spaces of historic towns and cities visually and suggested this as the basis for new planning and architecture using mixed forms, materials and functions. John Hewitt noted the 'Venetian intimacy' of Shelton Square.[40] The buildings around the square were faced in buff brick with decorative yellow brick parapets and white Portland stone to the six-storey office block. The office block (1958–60), designed in association with Ardin & Brookes of London was supported on six slender double-height mosaic-clad columns behind which were two levels of shops (Fig 36). The upper level was reached by a grand stair ascending from the square (now demolished) and a circular pool and fountain animated the space.

Figure 36
Office block and shops, Shelton Square (Arthur Ling, city architect and planning officer, and Ardin & Brookes, 1958–60). The fountain and the external stair to the first-floor shops have been removed. [DP164650]

Figure 37
City Market (Arthur Ling, city architect and planning officer, 1956–8). Tapering concrete columns around the central ring lit from the clerestory window.
[DP059615]

The City Market (1956–8, now listed Grade II)[41] was hidden behind Shelton Square, the Arcade and the Lower Precinct and attached to an existing three-storey factory building (Cornercroft, formerly the Victoria Building, now demolished) on Queen Victoria Road, the ground floor of which was converted to become the fish market.[42] The new market was 276ft (84.1m) in diameter and, uniquely, constructed from exposed in situ concrete with V-shaped columns and radial beams. The 160 fixed wooden stalls were arranged concentrically with another 40 stalls set in the outside wall, 16 of them facing outwards. The great space was lit through a raised clerestory above the central ring of columns and a continuous clerestory around the perimeter. The central ring (Fig 37) formed 'an eye about which the storm of salesmanship rages' and the circular layout gave 'the feeling of gorgeous confusion'.[43] The raw interior was decorated with Socialist Realist murals of farming and industry provided by art students from Dresden (Fig 38). A curved ramp on the north side (now demolished and replaced with bridges to adjacent car parks) led to a rooftop car park for 200 cars. It was connected by a bridge to the parking above the Arcade and the west

Figure 38
City Market, Socialist realist mural representing agriculture painted by art students from the city of Dresden, c 1958.
[DP059641]

side of Market Way and a further bridge above the offices linked to the east side
of Market Way and through to the Barracks car park (Fig 39). A square brick lift
tower (now demolished), surmounted by a clock held in a steel frame, marked
the service entrance from Queen Victoria Road but, otherwise, was only visible
when driving across the roofs of the city.

The entertainments precinct and Belgrade Theatre

Corporation Street, in what Gibson had planned as the entertainments precinct, was lined on the north side with banks and offices set behind arcades, on the pattern set by the Co-op, since it was clear from the mid-1950s that only one theatre was viable. Cinema audiences were in steep decline due to the popularity of television, and the pre-war Gaumont, Jordan Well (now part of Coventry University) and Empire, Hertford Street (rebuilt 1971–3) were still operating. The new Belgrade Theatre (1955–8, now listed Grade II),[44] named for a gift from the city of Belgrade of beech timber for interior ceilings, was intended as a venue for progressive, left-wing productions and to 'explore issues of cultural, social, political and moral significance'.[45] It was the first municipal theatre to be opened since the war and, with productions of plays by Arnold Wesker and David Turner, became a significant symbol for the new Coventry.[46]

The front to Corporation Street contained six small shops as well as the box office and foyer entrance, all set behind an arcade with flats for visiting actors above (Fig 40). The intention had been to bury the auditorium behind but, with the demand for shops satisfied, Ling introduced Belgrade Square, a new square

Figure 39 (opposite)
City Market and, left, the Cornercroft building (Arthur Ling, city architect and planning officer, 1956–8).
[Coventry City Council 1961, 36;
© Coventry City Council]

Figure 40 (right)
Belgrade Theatre, Corporation Street (Arthur Ling, city architect and planning officer, 1955–8).
[DP164973]

at the same scale as Shelton Square, with a free-standing *porte cochère* to the theatre and a fountain, and revealed the east elevation and foyer.[47] The northern boundary of the square was defined by Newsam's motor showroom with flats above (now demolished) and its east side by Upper Well Street and the *Coventry Evening Telegraph (CET)* office (1956–60), by L A Culliford & Partners, continuing the arcade eastwards (Fig 41). The *CET* and the offices to the west, the Amalgamated Engineering Union headquarters (1961) by J Roland Sidwell & Partners of Coventry, were clad in Gibson's Westmorland slate and travertine similar to the Upper Precinct whereas the Belgrade was significantly different. Ling's office was alive to many contemporary sources: the wedge form of the auditorium and boxy fly tower were influenced by the Kharkov theatre project of 1930[49] by the Bauhaus architect Marcel Breuer; the rich interior of the auditorium with its stepped side boxes, timber panelling and exterior of Portland stone are reminiscent of the 1951 Festival Hall; the Corporation Street elevation with its red brick framed in Portland stone, regular rectangular windows, projecting coffee bar window and round mosaic-clad columns is a smaller

Figure 41
Coventry Evening Telegraph *office, Upper Well Street and Corporation Street (L A Culliford & Partners, 1956–60).*
[DP164672]

version of Ralph Tubbs' Indian Students' Hostel in Fitzroy Square, London (1948–52), a building which defined 1950s civic design. The theatre also integrated applied art: the front was adorned with a *ciment fondu* relief of Belgrade by James Brown, an architect in Ling's department; in the foyers, the painter Martin Froy designed a mural of the 'Four Seasons' in Swedish and Italian tesserae; the spiral lights were designed by Bernard Schottlander, a German-born émigré who had trained at Leeds School of Art.

The civic precinct

The layout of the civic precinct along Little Park Street followed the principles set out in Gibson's 1944 model and 1945 plan of setting buildings in a landscape, except that the Beaux-Arts formality was now dropped. The first buildings – the Police Station (1954–7)[49] at the south end adjacent to the ring road and the Civic Offices (1951–7) at the north end facing Earl Street were started under Gibson and completed under Ling. Between them, Ling proposed law courts and a circular civic hall set within a landscape planned as a series of 'outdoor rooms'. The 'processional way' of Little Park Street remained as an avenue and the four-storey Telephone Exchange (1955) by the Ministry of Works, opposite the Police Station, defined its more formal southern entrance. As in the shopping precincts, Ling proposed towers at the southern end of Little Park Street to block the 'view of Victorian suburban houses', at the east end of Jordan Well by the Gaumont 'straddling the road [to] close the view and give a more definite setting for the Art Gallery and Museum' and at the north end of Priory Street to obscure 'a nondescript area of small factories and houses'. The idea is similar to the Swedish satellite town of Vällingby (1952–4), an important prototype of progressive planning, where some 15 point blocks encircled the town centre. Additionally, Ling, an expert on Soviet architecture and planning, would have known of Stalin's 1947 Moscow plan which placed 'wedding cake' towers at significant points of the city. For Ling:

> All these projects will add excitement to the bustling skyline of the central area, giving a real sense of architectural climax which corresponds to the social significance of the buildings.[50]

The Police Station and Civic Offices were both courtyard buildings, and both mainly faced in brick with low-pitched copper roofs, the style set by Gibson in sketch designs from 1950.[51] The Police Station has a more domestic scale and the detailing – the diaper brickwork and serpentine concrete walls of the assembly hall, the simple repeat windows and, particularly, the offset balconies of the west gable of the administration block – relate it to contemporary Danish architecture, and to the work of C F Møller at Aarhus University (Fig 42). The Civic Offices were arranged around a more formal rectilinear courtyard with a reflecting pool, circular fountain and willow trees and beautifully paved in concrete slabs and granite setts, intended as an exemplar of different landscaping materials. The Gibson buildings on the south and west sides were of plain brick but the façade facing Little Park Street was clad in timber boarding between Hornton stone pilasters, a variation from the travertine of the Police Station administration block. The second phase, enclosing the north and east sides of the courtyard (1958–60),[52] contained the Architecture and Planning Department (Fig 43). The north wing was raised on round concrete columns clad in diamond-set white mosaic to form an undercroft containing a glass kiosk for the public exhibition of current city projects and a city model. The offices above were fully glazed in an elegant aluminium curtain wall with milky glass

Figure 42
Police Station, Little Park Street (Donald Gibson, city architect and planning officer, 1954–7). Behind, the municipal offices (1971–3, left; see Fig 65) and the Severn Trent Water operations centre by Associated Architects of Birmingham (2008–12, right), herald the later density of the city.
[DP164726]

Figure 43
Courtyard of the Architecture and Planning
Department, Earl Street (Arthur Ling, city architect
and planning officer, 1958–60). The fully glazed upper
floors of the drawing offices raised on columns above
the exhibition kiosk.
[DP172626]

spandrel panels, a significant technical advance, to give natural light to the drawing offices. In the basement, a 15th-century medieval cellar, discovered during construction, was incorporated as the Crypt Club which became the social centre of the department, key to the camaraderie of the staff and to Ling's informal, 'democratic' management style.

Opposite, Sir Alfred Herbert's neoclassical Art Gallery, begun just before the war, was abandoned with only the basement completed (to become, first, public lavatories and, much later, a bar). The original donation proved too small and the City offered an alternative site to the east with additional funds and was therefore able to dictate a revised, more modern design and incorporate a museum. The new building (1954–60, altered) by Herbert, Son and Sawday of Leicester (Albert Herbert was a cousin of Sir Alfred) was a plain three-storey Blockley brick box, contained by transverse wings. The east wing was decorated in diaper brickwork and Portland stone sculpted panels; the west raised on Hornton stone piers to form an undercroft entrance and, between, a handsome steel-framed stair projected towards Earl Street. Although the Herbert was the first municipal gallery in Britain to be completed after the war, already this sort of design seemed out of date, especially when compared to the Civic Offices completed the same year. The same may be said of the row of five shops and flats on the south side of Earl Street completed under Gibson's regime and adjoining the Civic Offices. Gibson's consistent materials and delightful, small-scale details were rejected by Ling's generation in favour of bolder concepts and bigger statements.

The opportunity for these arose with the rest of the civic precinct, from Earl Street north to Fairfax Street and east across Cox Street to the ring road, taking in the area zoned in the 1945 plan for 'clubs'. As the MTCP had predicted in 1944, the area was far too big for municipal functions but, fortunately, both Coventry College of Art and Lanchester College of Technology[53] required new buildings and the area was redesignated. A site north of the Herbert was reserved for a new municipal library and the plan for swimming baths on Fairfax Street, first suggested in the 1939 plan, was revived. The scale and setting of the buildings were now defined by Basil Spence's new cathedral, won in competition in 1951 and under construction from 1955, with its nave running north–south and great porch marking a new entrance route connecting to Gibson's main city axis. The Central Swimming Baths (1956, built 1962–6, now listed Grade II)[54] was fitted on the narrow, sloping site between Cope Street and Fairfax Street (Fig 44). This produced a logical, linear arrangement of the three pools facing south and the entrance, changing rooms and spectators' gallery ranged along on

Figure 44
Perspective of the Central Swimming Baths from Cope Street drawn by James C Brown in 1963 (Arthur Ling, city architect and planning officer, 1956, constructed 1962–6).
[Reproduced with permission of the Herbert Art Gallery and Museum; © Culture Coventry]

the north side. The north and flank walls were clad in brick but the whole south side consisted of a glazed wall of heroic proportions folded outwards to form an angled bay around the diving pool. This and the contiguous main pool were covered symmetrically by a vast 'W'-shaped roof made of lattice steelwork supported on just four exposed steel columns. Its fascias were clad in stainless steel, its soffits, high above the pool, in aluminium. It appeared detached like a great wing flying above the horizontal mass of the building; the bright glass façade set against the stepped sunbathing terraces and gardens below Cope Street were an effective foil to Spence's solid sandstone nave. *Coventry New Architecture* reported in 1969:

> Coventry has been provided with one of the finest swimming pools in the world. It probably has no equal in Europe, and local pride has reason to be satisfied. ... [it] outclasses any of the other recently erected buildings in central Coventry and constitutes an exciting addition to the rebuilt city.[55]

The buildings of Lanchester College were set parallel to Cox Street and Cope Street, almost parallel to the cathedral nave (Fig 45). As suggested in 1944, a landscape ran between them, now revised to 'outdoor rooms' incorporating old

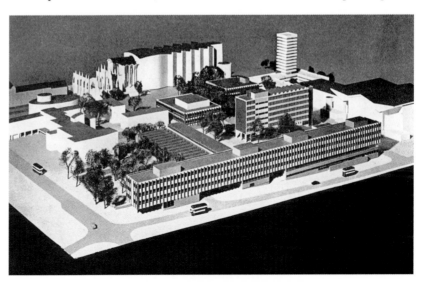

Figure 45
Model of the civic and cultural precinct (Arthur Ling, city architect and planning officer, c 1957). The site enclosed by Spence's cathedral, the Herbert Art Gallery and Museum, left, and Swimming Baths, right. The teaching block (1957–60) with the sawtooth roof is surrounded by the square Students' Union (1957–64) and Administration and Library (1957–64), the Workshop (1957–63) and the long Laboratory (1957–63) parallel to Cox Street.
[Johnson-Marshall 1966, 311, Plate 21;
© Edinburgh University Press]

trees and a graveyard with headstones, with a square, drawn to resemble the Campo in Siena, planned on the east side of the Cathedral. The exemplar university campus in the minds of the designers was Mies van der Rohe's Illinois Institute of Technology, celebrated for its gridded plan and consistent architectural vocabulary adapted for different building types. Except for the seven-storey teaching block (1950, built 1957–60)[56] on Cox Street (the three-storey flank wing of which was the temporary Art College opened in 1954), all the buildings were clad with glass and painted steel panels set between regularly spaced projecting steel I-beam mullions, a detail invented and made famous by Mies. Just as Mies had demonstrated, changes in ground level and basements were accommodated by setting the glazed walls on plinths, of brick in the Coventry version. The square Students' Union (1957–64, now FoundationCampus, altered) opposite the cathedral nave, rectangular Administration and Library building (1957–64, now Alan Berry Building, altered) facing the cathedral porch and linear Workshop (1957–63, demolished)[57] all had two-storey glazing. Most impressive of these was the 560ft (170.7m) long Laboratory (1957–63, now James Starley Building, altered) along Cox Street where a three-storey glazed wall sat on an almost windowless plinth, single storey at the south end and two-storey at the north (Fig 46). At the south, the curtain wall cantilevered far out beyond the brick; in the middle, an opening cut through the plinth connected the street to the campus gardens and the route to the Cathedral.

Having successfully established a style for the new campus, it would have seemed logical to adapt it for the remainder of the buildings on the site, especially as the Mies buildings in Chicago provided suitable precedents. That this did not happen reflects the diversity of the design groups within Ling's department and their limited expertise with the new technology of large-scale curtain walls. By this time Ling's political bosses were perhaps more interested in production than quality. The hall of residence for Lanchester College (1963–6, now Priory Hall)[58] was the only one of Ling's terminal blocks to be built in the civic precinct and the tallest in the city (Fig 47). The first proposal, for a smaller version of Mercia House with similar white horizontal bands and a podium aligned to the west end of the Baths, was relegated to a later phase. The 20-storey tower built between it and the Cathedral was made of grey aggregate-faced precast concrete panels using the Bison Wall Frame system, selected for its

low cost and speed of construction. It was a striking contrast to the sandstone walls of the Cathedral although the Royal Fine Art Commission, the Cathedral Council and Spence himself had approved the design. The tower had few architectural pretentions beyond its compact, symmetrical plan and height, presumably intended to counterbalance the Cathedral and baths. Only its vertical concrete ribs, terminating in futuristic angled fins gave it the 'interesting' profile Ling required and that was best seen from afar. Perhaps the fins were suggested by Spence's cathedral chapels and the tower has a marked similarity to Spence's 30-storey Hyde Park Cavalry Barracks in London which was being designed at the same time.[59] The halls signalled the end of the elegant Miesian aesthetic and of Scandinavian brickwork and the beginning of a new era of large-scale concrete buildings in the city.

Spon End and Hillfields and the tower blocks

The old Victorian suburbs of Spon End, west of the city centre, and Hillfields, to its north-east, both just outside the ring road, were bomb damaged and, although not classified as slums, presented a 'drab and depressing appearance'.[60]

Both were included in Gibson's development plan of 1951 as new neighbourhoods of low-rise, low-density housing with primary schools, businesses and open space similar to his peripheral suburbs. Wellington Gardens, Spon End (1948–52) had been developed with delightfully straightforward bungalows for old people, a short two-storey terrace and a community centre (now demolished), built of yellow brick with low-pitched copper roofs around a 'village' green (Fig 48). It was not until 1957, however, that both areas were declared Comprehensive Development Areas (allowing compulsory purchase) and were replanned by Ling's department with 4-storey, 10-storey and 17-storey flats. The increase in density was prompted by a fear of a future land shortage for housing and by generous government housing grants based on acreage (Spon End was 38 acres (15.4ha), Hillfields 139 acres (56.2ha)) and, from 1955 to 1966, government subsidies which increased progressively according to density. Ambitious annual housing targets were a key component of local Labour Party policies and these were more easily achieved through building flats rather than houses. In addition, the building industry was able to offer the City 'systems' (like Bison Wall Frame) for high-rise buildings and Ling brought practical experience from the LCC of designing flats.

Figure 48
Old people's housing, Wellington Gardens, Spon End (Donald Gibson, city architect and planning officer, 1948–52).
[DP164750]

Although the Ministry of Housing and Local Government did not recommend high-rise building over any other form, it did condone it. Ling would have agreed with Dame Evelyn Sharp, deputy secretary to the MHLG, that:

> from the point of view of the urban scene, high dwellings interspersed with low and middle-sized dwellings are really a thing of beauty. There is nothing it seems to me more appalling, more deadening in the urban landscape than a uniform mass of low buildings covering acres and acres.[61]

The ten-storey blocks consisted of flats and two-floor maisonettes arranged so that the access balconies and the lift served only the second, fifth and eighth floors. The open access balconies on the back, the central stair core and the sectional arrangement were clearly expressed between the grids of the exposed concrete frame. A pattern of projecting balconies and coloured panels on the front, patterned tiles at the entrances and a swallow wing roof canopy enlivened the form. At Spon End (1958–61), these blocks were used to create the north side of courtyards with four-storey blocks of maisonettes forming the other sides. The courtyards were planted with trees and there was some attempt to produce private enclosures and an urban form against Butts Road. At Hillfields, however, nine blocks (starting with Phoenix House completed in 1960, and now demolished with six others)[62] were arranged in echelon between Primrose Hill Street and Stoney Stanton Road with an open landscape between (Fig 49). Two further blocks were built south of Yardley Street (one now demolished). Phoenix House was intended to terminate the view down Trinity Street from Broadgate and the idea was to form 'town squares' with four-storey blocks similar to Spon End which, according to Ling, would 'give these lower lying areas a new importance'.[63] By 1962, the project had been revised with a 30-storey tower north-east of the Swanswell and the pedestrianisation of the whole area from Raglan Street to Stoney Stanton Road, erasing White Street and Primrose Hill Street. By 1969, none of this had materialised and *Coventry New Architecture* noted of Hillfields that 'no attempt at human scaling appears to have been made, and the bulldozer has been given free rein among the terraces'.[64] Especially difficult was the design of car parking – either grouped into desolate garage courtyards or distributed on oceans of tarmac on all sides of the buildings. At Hillfields, the ten-storey blocks were loosely composed against two 17-storey

Figure 49 (left)
Paul Stacy House, Hillfields estate, Victoria Street (Arthur Ling, city architect and planning officer, c 1960).
[DP164760]

Figure 50 (below)
Meadow House, Spon Street, Spon End (Arthur Ling, city architect and planning officer, c 1960–4).
[DP164747]

tower blocks, Pioneer House and Thomas King House, and another, Meadow House (intended to be the centre of a dense grid of four-storey flats), was built at the north of the Spon End site, against the ring road (Fig 50). These were of similar designs, square or almost square in plan with continuous solid concrete balconies to each floor, dark-tiled panels between adjacent flats and heavier roof parapets with cut away slotted corners. Each contained about 95 one- and two-bedroomed flats intended for families without children. The towers stood as 'markers' to locate the estates on the skyline of the city and, as with the city centre, other significant points on the outside of the ring road were marked with similar towers. Three – Naul's Mill House, Samuel Vale House and William Batchelor House – marked the northern routes out of the city and the Coventry canal basin (Fig 51). These tucked surprisingly easily into the existing grain of old brick buildings and William Batchelor House demonstrated how a private landscape could be preserved and cars could be accommodated by building a sweeping, defensive brick garage against the ring road.

Figure 51
Naul's Mill House, Samuel Vale House and William Batchelor House marking the routes to the northern part of the city beyond the ring road (Arthur Ling, city architect and planning officer, c 1960–4).
[DP164734]

Ling was also concerned with the remoteness of the new neighbourhoods of Tile Hill, Willenhall and Bell Green and how they could be connected to the new city centre through the 'monotony of [the] subtopian belt' of inter-war suburbs. He suggested that the radial routes could be widened, planted with trees and redeveloped to 'pull the whole city together'.[65] To the motorist, this would give the impression that the whole of Coventry had been redeveloped; the isolation of the new suburbs would be removed and the morale of those who lived in the subtopia would be boosted by the adjacent new buildings. In the event, none of the three routes was developed comprehensively. However, the route to Bell Green along Stoney Stanton Road and Bell Green Road was marked, like milestones, with two 17-storey blocks, Falkener House, at the bend at Great Heath, and Longfield House, at Courthouse Green, and by a ten-storey block at Eden Street (1961) before terminating at Riley Square with another 17-storey tower, Dewis House (1961–5). It was town planning on a grand scale, but perhaps rather too subtle for the subtopians to notice. Other towers seemed more serendipitous: John Fox House, Henley Green (1966–8, now Caradoc Hall, *see* p 80) was stranded in the middle of the green of the predominantly two-storey Manor Farm Estate; Alpha House, Stoke Heath (1962–3)[66] related to the narrow strip of open land of Barras Heath but was surrounded by two-storey pitch roof inter-war terraces (Fig 52). Alpha House was built as the prototype for the Costain Jackblock system of construction where finished floors were built at ground level and jacked into position. Dewis House used a similar system developed by British Lift Slab and John Fox House used the Truscon patent system of steel reinforcement. With all of them the designs were led more by construction engineering and economics than by the imaginative hands of Ling's department, although *Coventry New Architecture* praised Alpha House for the repeated patterns of its black and grey cladding panels.

The ring road and Railway Station

After the completion of Shelton Square the necessity of building the ring road to allow the city centre to become free of through traffic and more pedestrianised became acute. The first section of the road, from the junction of London Road to the junction of New Union Street next to the Police Station (1959), and the second, from Foleshill Road west to Radford Road (1961) were completed to Gibson's original layout – a dual carriageway at ground level with wide reservations for cycle paths and roundabouts at the junctions. By that time, however, predicted traffic densities had greatly increased and the 'science' of traffic engineering was firmly established, influenced by American experience and home-grown examples like Stevenage, Birmingham and the Chiswick flyover completed by 1959. The problem was that Gibson's roundabouts impeded traffic flow to the radial routes and on the ring road itself, exacerbated by the closeness of the junctions. Ling and the city engineer and surveyor, Granville Berry, completely revised the design by 1961 to become, in effect, Britain's first urban motorway. Their analysis of predicted traffic flows and destinations was given added status by the pioneering use of the largest IBM computer in the country.[67] Except at Foleshill Road, the roundabouts were replaced with slip roads and the junctions became grade-separated, greatly increasing the overall width of the road and the area of the junctions. The cycle paths and Gibson's setting of the road in a linear park disappeared. Except along its southern perimeter where it dipped below Warwick Road, the road was

Figure 52
Alpha House, Barras Green, Barras Heath (Arthur Ling, city architect and planning officer, c 1962–3). [DP164828]

mostly elevated but, with the slip roads, it formed an almost impenetrable barrier around the inner city, limiting both vehicular and pedestrian connections. The western side was completed in two phases (1962–6) and the eastern side in three phases (1968–74) (Fig 53). The final phase which reconstructed the first phase, narrowly missing the Police Station between two spaghetti-like flyovers, was completed in 1974. Appropriately, the theme of the RIBA Conference held in Coventry in 1962 was 'Building and Planning for the Motor Age'. The conference was addressed by Colin Buchanan (1907–2001), an influential architect/planner who was reporting to the Minister of Transport, Ernest Marples, on the problems of traffic in urban areas and who had been working with the Coventry planners. Buchanan's seminal book *Traffic in Towns* (1963) warned that 'it is not difficult to have misgivings about the circumferential severance of the [Coventry] city centre' and that because of the paucity of car parking in the centre, Coventry was 'very far from being 'fully motorized' in the sense of freedom to use cars' and, therefore, of the 'absolute necessity' of maintaining public transport.[68] *Traffic in Towns* was welcomed by the Planning Department and all members of the Planning and Redevelopment Committee received a copy.[69] Regardless, the design of the ring road remained unaffected.

The severance of the centre from the outer areas by the ring road was solved by constructing pedestrian bridges and underpasses at strategic points. Some of the bridges, for example on the route from the railway station, were at grade but others and including the underpasses required tortuous and uncomfortable detours. For example, the key strategic route from Spon Street to Spon End, marked across the ring road by Meadow House, dived into a dimly lit, narrow underpass with steps and ramps. The ring road ate into public spaces: Greyfriars Green was greatly reduced; Lady Herbert's Gardens and almshouses, founded by Sir Alfred as a memorial to his wife in 1930 and containing part of the 14th-century city wall, found themselves crammed up against Swanswell Ringway. Apart from the civic gardens along Little Park Street, these became the only green spaces in the city centre. The spaces under the road were used for car parking or, at White Street, for parking coaches. Volgograd Place, the interlocking fountains set in cobbles under the ring road at White Street (1970, now derelict), designed by Douglas Smith Stimson Partnership of Leicester, failed to ameliorate the dank, claustrophobic route to Hillfields (Fig 54). The universal criticism of the noise of urban roads was avoided, however, simply

Figure 53
Swanswell and Whitefriars elevated sections of the ring road looking south-east (Arthur Ling, city architect and planning officer, and Granville Berry, city engineer, 1961, constructed 1968–74). William Batchelor House, foreground, with Lady Herbert's Gardens opposite and the bus station and Fairfax Street beyond. Swanswell Pool on the east side with the massive Wheatley Street Bus Garage (Harry Noble, city architect and planning officer, 1982–3), beyond.
[26495_002]

Figure 54
Volgograd Place, Hales Street/White Street, under the
Swanswell interchange (Douglas Smith of Douglas
Smith Stimson Partnership, 1970). The circular
fountains derelict in 2014.
[DP164679]

because there were no residents left in the city centre to complain except those in
the red brick Victorian terraces of Starley Road which had been truncated and
turned into a cul-de-sac.

Because of delays and uncertainties with the new railway station, the bus
station was located on Pool Meadow where it had been placed in the 1939 plan,
as far from the railway station as possible. The Railway Station (1958–62, now
listed Grade II) by W R Headley, regional architect to British Railways Midland
Region, placed a great concrete table-top roof at right angles to the tracks
creating a double height booking hall, containing the stairs, lifts and bridges and
forming a *porte cochère* to Station Square (Fig 55). This bold statement was
delicately detailed with thin aluminium-framed windows, white tile walls,
varnished timber boarded ceilings and a little planted courtyard to the snack bar

and waiting room on platform 1. Station Square contained a 16-storey office tower, Copthall House (1962–5, demolished), by W H Saunders & Son, another of Ling's markers outside the ring road (Fig 56). This was clad all-round in a silver anodised aluminium curtain wall, a style then becoming universal for urban office towers around the world, much influenced by American practice

Figure 55
Coventry Railway Station, Station Square (W R Headley, regional architect to British Railways Midland Region, 1958–62).
[DP164744]

and aided in Britain by the pioneering glass company Pilkington's. More interesting was the low, long five-storey block of offices (now demolished) clad in horizontal bands of grey slate, the first building designed to face the ring road and accept the larger scale that this demanded (Fig 57). A great two-storey 'gateway' under the building marked the entrance to the square and the route to the city centre across the traffic-filled gulf below. Comparison with the Police Station, designed only ten years before and in the context of a much smaller boulevard, is very telling and an indication of the future scale of the city.

Figure 56 (above)
Copthall House office tower, Station Square
(W H Saunders & Son, 1962–5).
[DP164745]

Figure 57 (above, right)
Copthall House north block, Station Square/
Manor Road (W H Saunders & Son, 1962–5).
[DP164746]

5

Gregory and the completion of the plan 1964–73

Concrete panels on the wall of the Three Tuns public house, Bull Yard (William Mitchell, sculptor, 1966). [DP164663]

Figure 58 (below)
Terence Gregory photographed in 1973 in his office on Earl Street. In the background the old and new cathedrals, the halls of Lancester College and, right, the first phase of the Library attached to the Herbert Art Gallery and Museum.
[00752625; © Mirrorpix]

Ling left Coventry in 1964, perhaps sensing that his strategic planning work was completed. He was already working privately on a development plan for Claverdon village (1960–2) and on the master plan for the University of Warwick (from 1958 with Stewart Johnston and 1964 with Alan Goodman). He strongly believed that the new university should be sited within the city, and became disillusioned when the peripheral site was chosen. He was appointed professor of Architecture and Civic Planning (1964–9) and professor of Environmental Design (1969–72) at Nottingham University and set up a private planning consultancy. He was architect/planner for Runcorn new town (1965–67) and president of the Royal Town Planning Institute (1968–9) but, like Gibson, his reputation was made by Coventry. Ling may also have foreseen that the local Labour Party, which had consistently supported his ideas for ten years, was on the wane. Membership had declined through the 1950s and Labour's share of the local vote steadily fell until it lost the municipal election of 1967 to the Conservatives, ending its 30-year rule of the city. This was due to a number of factors. Locally, the party had failed to attract youth and young homeowners, who now represented a substantial and affluent new working class, and it had also lost the automatic support of local shop stewards, who were an essential link to canvassing factory workers. The mid-1960s saw unprecedented annual rate increases and, as the pioneering days of reconstruction faded in local memory, housing estates became more established, unemployment remained low and luxury goods easily attainable, Coventrians were less willing to pay for the final phases of their city. Nationally, the Labour government's emergency budget of July 1966 which restricted public investment and hire purchase, increased petrol duty and 'froze' all wages and prices was deeply unpopular and the 1967 elections were the first opportunity for voters to express their views. Bristol, Cardiff, Leeds, Liverpool, Manchester, Newcastle, Nottingham and Wolverhampton as well as Coventry lost their Labour administrations. George Hodgkinson, then aged 74, was not re-elected as Alderman and retired from politics.

On Ling's recommendation, his replacement was his deputy, Terence Gregory (1919–2000), an architect-planner who had joined Coventry in 1960 (Fig 58). Gregory had graduated from the Birmingham School of Architecture in 1939 and finished his studies after the war at the Wolverhampton and Staffordshire Technical College. He had been chief assistant architect at

Wolverhampton Borough (1949–54) and deputy city architect and estates manager at Gloucester City from 1954. Gregory was well liked, a consummate organiser and committee stalwart but not an innovator; his task was not to replan the city but to finish, under increasing financial restrictions, what Ling had started. He completed the blocks of Hillfields, but only a few of the shops in the square at the foot of Pioneer House were built, leaving intact the existing shops in the 19th-century terraces along Victoria Street. At Spon End, the four-storey blocks of maisonettes (1970) below Meadow House were built as cheaply as possible in precast concrete panels with deck access and common stairways supported on concrete legs (Fig 59). It was the first high density housing in the city to have its own multi-deck parking (now demolished). Notwithstanding the decent proportions of the courtyards, the crude architectural detail and lack of private space failed to achieve the promise of earlier schemes. Potentially more exciting was the very much denser St Austell Road Estate, Wyken (1965–7) with a mixture of four-storey flats, old people's housing, two-storey family houses in courtyards and two big blocks of flats of 10 and 15 storeys. The flats

Figure 59
Four-storey maisonettes, Spon End (Terence Gregory, city architect and planning officer, c 1970).
[DP164752]

Figure 60
Vincent Wyles House, Attoxhall Road, St Austell Road estate, Wyken (Terence Gregory, city architect and planning officer, 1965–7).
[DP164813]

were perched in echelon on the highest part of the site and clad in grey concrete (Fig 60). Their inspiration may have been the slabs of the London County Council's Alton West estate (themselves based on Le Corbusier's Unité d'Habitation block in Marseille), but here they remained stuck to the ground with blank brickwork panels instead of pilotis, the same regular windows and balconies on every elevation and the flat roof unused, despite the exceptional view. They were the last of Coventry's high-rise flats.

Completing the civic precinct and Lanchester Polytechnic

Gregory was more successful with his extensions to the civic precinct. The project for the Lanchester Polytechnic halls of residence next to Coventry Baths was revived. The new 13-storey tower and podium now looked rather diminutive next to its 20-storey neighbour and the spaces around it somewhat confused. However, the new square, Cathedral Square, formed against the north end of the Cathedral with the De Vere Hotel (1972–3, now Britannia Hotel) by G R Stone & Associates on its west side (Fig 61), completed the sequence of

Figure 61
De Vere Hotel (now Britannia Hotel), Cathedral Square,
Fairfax Street (G R Stone & Associates, 1972–3).
[DP164970]

spaces through the polytechnic and resolved the difficult problem of the setting of the Lady Chapel.[70] The hotel bridged Fairfax Street, suggesting the form and scale for later buildings to the north, shown in a 1972 model as office blocks and an entertainment area above a multi-storey car park and bus station. The six-storey linear block of halls (1969–74, now Quadrant Hall),[71] facing Fairfax Street, was lifted high above the ground to allow the road to join Fairfax Street on its way to the bus station and to make the visual termination of Priory Street that Ling had wanted (Fig 62). Both the halls and hotel were made of concrete panels following the precedent of the first tower. The hotel was plain and linear, whereas Gregory articulated the halls around five cores capped with heavy pyramidal zinc roofs and clearly expressed the concrete cross walls and strip windows (made from light green plastic). The result is a more interesting architecture, which, in common with much of the contemporary work from his department, took on a new, massive scale more appropriate to its siting near to the ring road. Nowhere is this approach clearer than in the Sports and Recreation Centre (1973–6)[72] built above Cox Street between the baths and the ring road (Fig 63). Known affectionately as the 'elephant', the massive,

Figure 62
Quadrant Hall, Fairfax Street (Terence Gregory, city architect and planning officer, 1969–74). [DP164971]

Figure 63
Sports and Recreation Centre, Fairfax Street and Cox Street (Terence Gregory, city architect and planning officer, 1973–6). The glazed bridge links through to the Central Swimming Baths. [DP164685]

apparently windowless building was formed as a series of abstract prisms extending to the ground with tapered legs, all clad in grey zinc. The entrance is by a thin glass bridge connected at first-floor level to the baths; the black undercroft is for vehicles only. Its brave concept is more reminiscent of the futuristic, vertically separated city of Buchanan's *Traffic in Towns* than Gibson or Ling's picturesque visions of a human-scaled, horizontally separated city.

The embryo of this idea may be seen in the Art College (1966–7, now Graham Sutherland Building)[73] which replaced the unfinished building along Cope Street planned by Gibson, built by Ling and absorbed into the technical college (Fig 64). Under Gregory, a new site was found between Cox Street and the ring road. Servicing was concealed on the lower ground floor against the slip road and the main pedestrian entrance was up steps over the roof of the printing workshops. These formed an irregular, sawtoothed plinth of dark brick, taking up the angle of the ring road and presenting a blank façade to Gosford Street. It was as if a bridge would one day connect back to the main campus and the ground levels would be abandoned to vehicles alone. Ling's Miesian

Figure 64
Art College (now Graham Sutherland Building), Cox Street/Gosford Street (Terence Gregory, city architect and planning officer, 1966–7. [DP164690]

Figure 65
Municipal offices, Meschede Way, between Little Park Street and Much Park Street (Terence Gregory, city architect and planning officer, 1971–3).
[DP164720]

façades also disappeared: on the lower four floors, the concrete columns were exposed and the glazing set back within dark-brown panels; the two floors above were set flush with the column faces and divided with projecting concrete mullions, five to each bay; the top floor projected slightly and was a blank set of concrete panels, concealing northlights within a parapet. It was a confident, monumental statement in line with the Brutalism then dominating the avant-garde of British architecture, distantly based on the elevational composition of Le Corbusier's monastery of La Tourette near Lyon (1957–60), and it is instructive to compare other contemporary derivatives such as Boston City Hall, Massachusetts (1963–8).

In the southern part of the civic precinct, Gregory added more municipal offices (1971–3)[74] in the form of a 15-storey tower, approached by foot through gardens from Little Park Street but separately serviced from the lower level of Much Park Street, akin to the arrangements of the Art College and Sports Centre. The tower was square on plan with continuous balconies at each level and of similar overall proportions to Mercia House (Fig 65). However, its elevations were articulated with chamfered corners and an external grid of white precast concrete mullions and handrails shading an inner, glazed curtain wall. At the entrance levels, the grid was reduced to eight flat concrete columns revealing the glazing behind; above the entrance and at roof level, it became more solid. It was the most elegant tower in the city and an effective foil to Gibson's pale brick, copper roofed courtyard to the north and termination for the informal, verdant pedestrian route that now wound its way across the city from Greyfriars spire and Ford's Hospital to Meschede Way.

Bull Yard, Hertford Street precinct and Coventry Point

Gregory completed Bull Yard (1963–9),[75] the extension of the shopping precinct from Shelton Square, with a 'C'-shaped set of shops facing outwards to New Union Street and connecting with Hertford Street and Warwick Road (Fig 66). The shops and Three Tuns public house marked a change of style, though the standard 20ft (6.1m) shop module was maintained. The first floor on all three sides of the square overhung the ground floor to form a canopy faced in closely

Figure 66
Bull Yard, Warwick Road/Hertford Street (Arthur Ling succeeded by Terence Gregory, city architect and planning officer, 1963–9). The white concrete fascia above the shops conceals the rooftop car parking. [DP164659]

spaced bronze-clad projecting mullions with glazed and black enamelled steel panels between. These contrasted with the white stone of Shelton Square and the white concrete of the parapet wall of the rooftop car park on the north side. The south parapet proclaimed 'BULL YARD' in a silhouetted, illuminated sign. The wall of the Three Tuns was embellished with vigorous cast concrete panels by the sculptor William Mitchell in his 'Aztec' style (now listed Grade II, *see* p 64) and, in the centre of the square, was a kiosk (now demolished) roofed with an overlarge fibreglass dome (now relocated to the Warwick Row underpass). The effect was sharp and contemporary, making it the most successful of all the entrances to the shopping precinct.

With the ring road almost complete, Gregory turned to the pedestrianisation of Hertford Street (1965–74), closing the road in 1969. All the shops on the north-west side were demolished and replaced with a simple stepped terrace of two-storey shops on the 20ft module with solid canopies (now replaced), like Market Street. These, together with the substantial office block squeezed between Hertford Street and the Barracks car park, were designed by W S Hattrell & Partners (Fig 67). Their only architectural

Figure 67
Hertford Street, north-west side (W S Hattrell &
Partners, 1965–74). The projecting canopies have
been changed from solid horizontal planes to pitched
glass. The sculpted panels to the first-floor elevations
are by William Mitchell. In the distance, the red-brick
façades of A D Foulkes shop (now the Litten Tree) by
Hellberg & Harris, 1956.
[DP164646]

distinction was the bronze fibreglass cladding of the upper floors of the shops and the concrete cladding panels of the office, designed in characteristic muscular, abstract forms by William Mitchell. The middle section of the road was raised to allow access from below to Barracks car park from Warwick Lane, another example of Gregory's vertical separation of the city, but necessitating ramps and steps for pedestrians. The middle section of the south-east side of the street was redesigned by Redgrave & Clarke with A J Fowles & Partners and this part was roofed with a glazed, concrete-beamed pergola. The upper shops, including the old Post Office and the National Provincial Bank, were retained to face a triangular place with Broadgate House and the rebuilt Empire (ABC) Cinema (1971–3) by Archer Boxer & Partners. This was in blank dark-blue brick with white concrete steps and balcony (now demolished) jutting into the place and giving access to the cinema above the shops. Hertford Street was the only long street in Coventry specifically designed for pedestrians, its width not determined by vehicles, and, except for the City Arcade, the centre section was the first covered shopping in the city. Although the intention was to reintroduce the supposed intimacy of the medieval street, the effect, especially in the covered area, was overwhelmingly claustrophobic since there were no side connections other than to the multi-level car park or the dreary service courts. Worst of all, the project proposed the filling in of the Broadgate House bridge with a two-storey bank, thereby blocking the view through Gibson's grand arch and reducing the access to two narrow alleyways.

Gregory found yet another site for a speculative office tower, Coventry Point (1969–75), on the north side of Barracks car park on Market Way where Ling had proposed a single tower hotel in 1962. This was wedged between Woolworth's, BHS, the Gas Board's showroom and the Market Tavern so that putting a building here at all required some architectural gymnastics and a very good structural engineer, Ove Arup & Partners. The building was designed by the John Madin Design Group of Birmingham and, in effect, was two towers linked with a glazed 'corridor' (actually more offices): one at 15 storeys in Market Way with an impossibly slim core and foyer (now altered) from which it cantilevered above the second floor; the other at 14 storeys with an entrance buried behind the Gas Board showroom and from the third floor of the car park (Fig 68). Both towers had white flint aggregate concrete panels, chamfered corners, pitched (glazed) roofs and expressive profiles, similar to the Lanchester tower, making it likely that Gregory's department had a major influence over the design. The probability of downdraughts from the tower onto Market Way was solved by building a steel space-frame canopy cantilevered from the office core, covering the street. Unfortunately, this made for a gloomy experience for the shopper and Gregory was forced to invent an 'area of brightness' with lots of lights attached to the underside of the canopy.[76] Here and in Hertford Street, it was as if the City was only interested in increasing its rateable value by

Figure 68
Coventry Point, Market Way seen across the roof of the Barracks car park (John Madin Design Group, 1969–75).
[DP164643]

exploiting every possible opportunity for lettable floor area and had forgotten Gibson or Mumford's high ideals of providing grand public spaces for activities other than commerce.

Dealing with old buildings

The construction of the ring road, the polytechnic, the Civic Offices and Hertford Street involved the destruction of many old buildings that had escaped bomb damage and were still serviceable. There was not much public protest. The only example of effective opposition was a petition from 47,000 citizens in 1961 which saved the lime and plane trees threatened by the proposed widening of Warwick Road.[77] The City Guild, which had been active in forming the post-war city, was largely silent from the mid-1950s and the Coventry Civic Amenity Society was not founded until 1970. Even when old buildings were not in the way of new development, there was a reluctance to reuse them. Rare exceptions included the paired Albert Building (now Iceland) and Cornercroft (formerly Victoria Building, now demolished) on Queen Victoria Road, the latter used as the fish market (the upper floors as a bowling alley and supermarket), and the new shop for A D Foulkes, homeware suppliers (1956, now the Litten Tree), by Hellberg & Harris on Warwick Road, which converted the Edwardian showroom of the Rover car company.[78] Significantly, both of these projects eliminated almost all traces of the original architecture and invented new façades in new materials. Ling inserted a recessed arcade into Albert and Cornercroft, covered the Victorian brick structure with Hornton stone, removed the parapets and reglazed the openings with a modern curtain wall. Hellberg & Harris replaced an ebullient baroque façade with the plainest red brick and small rectangular windows and added a projecting gallery intended to be part of the future covered way of Bull Yard (see Fig 67).

Only a few ancient buildings were restored after bomb damage, including the roof of St Mary's Hall (in 1953 by the city engineer), Ford's Hospital (1951–3, by W S Hattrell using salvaged timbers), Bond's Hospital and the red-brick 18th-century 11 Priory Row (1953, by A H Gardner & Partners) next to the new cathedral. The 1944 and 1947 Town and Country Planning Acts required local authorities to compile lists of buildings of 'special architectural or historic interest' for unique protection. Coventry's first lists did not appear until 1955, after the new precincts were firmly established, and concentrated on the major medieval churches including the cathedral ruins, monastic remains, the ruins of the city wall, the major medieval timber-framed buildings and Priory Row. No listed buildings were allowed to get in the way of new developments. Attitudes began to change in 1956 with the destruction, for the lack of funds to restore them, of a group of buildings containing a 14th-century roof adjoining Cheylesmore Manor gatehouse, south of New Union Street. The surviving gatehouse, listed Grade I in 1955 (but later downgraded to Grade II*), was restored by F W B Charles of Worcester, a specialist in the conservation of timber buildings, for use as the Registry Office (1966–8). Gregory added an extension (1968–72)[79] in striated dark-brown brick and glass, cleverly suggesting the proportions and tone of the old wattle and half-timbering without any hint of pastiche (Fig 69). On the north side, the extension folded around an intimate, beautifully scaled courtyard formed from the angled rear wing of the long office block (1969), designed by Hellberg Harris & Partners. This faced New Union Street, constructed in 1966, as part of the new 'professional' precinct (Fig 70). It was one of the best new façades of the city: a Gibson-esque arcade with tiled columns ran the full length of the brown brick block; the first-floor windows were of a tall, Georgian proportion, delicately modulated in each bay; the upper-floor windows ran in a continuous clerestory, perhaps suggested by the topshops (weavers' workshops) of old Coventry. An archway, marked by interrupting the pitched roof line, elongating the window proportions and quickening the arcade rhythm, connected through to the Registry Office courtyard. It was civilised, quiet and subtle – qualities that the new Hertford Street so obviously lacked.

Gregory was more sympathetic than Ling to the plight of Coventry's rapidly dwindling stock of ancient buildings. In 1965 he commissioned F W B Charles to survey all the remaining timber-framed buildings and his report revealed that only 34 survived from the 100 recorded by the National Buildings Record in 1958 and the 240 that had survived the war. A significant group remained in Spon Street, now rendered a cul-de-sac by the ring road, and here Gregory proposed the first 'Townscape Scheme', supported in principle by the Historic Buildings Council, to restore the houses and to re-erect buildings from Much Park Street threatened by redevelopment. This would form an 'historic' precinct

Figure 69
Registry Office, Cheylesmore Manor gatehouse,
Manor Yard, off New Union Street. Medieval building
restored by F W B Charles and new building by Terence
Gregory, city architect and planning officer, 1966–8.
[DP164730]

Figure 70
New Union Street offices, south side (Hellberg Harris
& Partners, 1969).
[DP164729]

with Bond's Hospital, Bablake School and St John's Church for tourists and specialised small shops, like Brighton's Lanes or York's Shambles. The moving of historic buildings had been suggested by Gibson for Ford's Hospital and had been proposed, but not carried out, in other cities like Plymouth and Bristol. The idea was enthusiastically supported by Charles who oversaw the first restorations from 1968 to 1975 and transferred 7–10 Much Park Street to become 163–4 Spon Street (1970–4; Fig 71). Charles's idea of restoration was

Figure 71
Nos 163–4 (left, three-storey), 166, 167–8 and 169 Spon Street. Medieval buildings restored by F W B Charles, 1970–4; 163–4 Spon Street was the relocated 7–10 Much Park Street but the others were pre-existing. [DP164668]

uniquely modernist. For him, the 'honesty' of expressing the medieval timber was everything; all other structure and materials, the accretions of age and the marks of successive centuries were removed and, when old timber was missing, new timber was used to his own designs, based on his academic study of contemporary structures. The critic Ian Nairn noted of Cheylesmore Manor that it 'seems likely to come out more half-timbered than it has been for centuries';[80] he was not wrong – Charles's restorations were unrecognisable as the muddled brick- and plaster-faced old buildings he had inherited. The effect of Spon Street was that of a museum of timber building types, straightened up and polished inside and out so that even the genuine parts looked new. Particularly unfortunate and unnecessary was the removal of all chimneystacks on the pretext that they were made of Georgian or Victorian bricks. The Spon Street buildings were listed Grade II in 1974 together with a large number of Victorian churches and other 19th-century buildings, Old County Hall and the Council House, both of which Ling had suggested demolishing. Spon Street and the area around Priory Row became the city's first Conservation Areas under the Civic Amenities Act of 1967. It showed how quickly architectural tastes had changed through the late 1960s and how the assumption of wholesale clearance that Gibson and Ling had operated under was now very out of date.

6

The suburbs

The blitz destroyed some 8,500 houses in Coventry, about 7 per cent of the total stock. A further two out of three houses were damaged, but, although most of these were repaired during the war, with the influx of workers to the wartime factories the waiting list for housing in 1945 stood at over 7,000, rising to almost 12,000 by the following year. The promise of good-quality housing for rent had helped secure the landslide victory of the 1945 Labour Government and became the preoccupation of Aneurin Bevan, the Minister for Health, whose policies ensured the local authorities a virtual monopoly of house building. Despite the 1,000 temporary prefabricated houses supplied by Government, there continued to be squatters and ad hoc encampments of caravans in the city centre, the last of which was not cleared from Little Park Street until 1953. The provision of houses and the building of the schools, libraries, clinics and community centres to support them became the main concern of the City Council and Gibson and Ling's departments from the 1940s until the mid-1960s. The idea of council housing was not new to Coventry: at the vast Radford estate, north-west of the city centre, 2,500 houses for rent had been built between the wars (Fig 72).

Manor Farm estate, Henley Road, Bell Green. (Arthur Ling succeeded by Terence Gregory, city architect and planning officer, 1964–7). Hermes Crescent runs around the perimeter; the 17-storey John Fox House (now Caradoc Hall) sits isolated in the greenspace between the dense blocks of houses. [29210_040]

Figure 72 (right)
The Radford Estate, late 1930s. Ribbon planning and short terraced houses with gardens accessed from a back lane. Shops grouped around Jubilee Crescent, centre. [29210_002]

George Hodgkinson had been the chairman of the Housing Committee from 1934 to 1936 under the Progressive administration and almost 4,000 houses had been built in 1936 alone, although most of these were by private developers exploiting an abundance of cheap labour. In 1937, Hodgkinson had approved the building of 1,000 council houses at Charter Avenue, Canley, south of the mainline railway and, when the Director of Housing, A F Underhill, retired in 1940, his department was transferred to the Architecture and Planning Department, giving Gibson his first mass housing project.

Gibson's first design for Canley, built on Sheriff Avenue (1940–1),[81] was of single and double pairs of semi-detached flat roof brick houses 'with the avoidance of any unusual and therefore distinctive lay-out pattern'[82] (Fig 73), while the remainder of the estate had standard pitched-roof brick houses in staggered rows (Mayor's Croft, Templars' Fields and Prior Deram Walk). Gibson's experience with traditional construction drove him to develop ideas of prefabrication from the Lache nursery school, prompted by his conviction, first mentioned in his lecture to the Royal Society of Arts in 1940 (and taking

Figure 73
Houses on Sheriff Avenue, Canley (Donald Gibson, city architect, 1940–1). Plain red brick with precast concrete porches with tiled decoration.
[DP164778]

inspiration from Gropius), that after the war engineering factories could turn to the production of houses, replacing conventional building materials and labour. In 1942, the Housing Committee commissioned a prototype 'Coventry' house and a second prototype, 'Radiation' house (Radiation, its sponsor, was a supplier of gas and coke) was developed in 1945 (Fig 74). Both had lightweight steel frames, precast concrete slab and asbestos sheet cladding, pitched roofs and prefabricated plumbing and heating. A third 'GBS Unibuilt' house, designed by the architects G Grey Wornum and Richard Sheppard, and part sponsored by the steel fabricators Brockhouse & Co of West Bromwich, was built at Canley in 1943.[83] However, further development was curtailed by the Government allocation, in 1946, of 2,000 British Iron & Steel Federation (BISF) Type 'A' houses, a similar prefabricated steel-framed system clad in corrugated steel designed by the architect Frederick Gibberd and engineer Donovan Lee. Gibson distributed these to Charter Avenue and 48 to the Stonebridge Highway estate where he planned a mixture of flats, courtyard houses and old people's bungalows.

Although the Stonebridge project started construction in 1947, by 1949 only the roads and drains were in place due to the chronic shortage of local

Figure 74
The 'Coventry' house under construction (Donald Gibson, city architect, 1942). Precast concrete slabs clipped to a slender steel frame.
[The Future Coventry, 30; © Coventry City Council]

skilled labour caused by the better conditions and wages in the engineering factories. The Government withdrew its offer of BISF houses and the City was forced to negotiate with George Wimpey, the national contractors, to use their 'no fines' system of construction.[84] The design was hastily rejigged to be flats only (1950–1) (Fig 75) although the original long, three-storey *zeilenbau* form of the blocks fanning out from Charminster Drive was retained.[85] Only 208 pairs of BISF houses were built at Charter Avenue (1946–7, between Bradney Green and Wolfe Road), set rigidly on an east–west orientation in stepped rows with open front lawns bisected by a grid of curvilinear access roads (Fig 76). The monotony of both estates was disappointing and the experience proved that, since the houses were architecturally modest, it would require imaginative layouts, varied density and a richer landscape to make distinctive places.

Figure 75
Flats, Fred Lee Grove, Stonebridge Highway estate (Donald Gibson, city architect and planning officer, 1950–1).
[DP164786]

Figure 76
BISF Type 'A' houses, Hancock Green, Canley (Frederick Gibberd, architect, and Donovan Lee, engineer. Layout by Donald Gibson, city architect, 1946–7).
[DP172655]

Theory and practice in the new suburbs – Tile Hill, Willenhall and Bell Green

Housing in the first new suburbs – at Tile Hill at the western edge of the city north of Canley, Willenhall at the south-east, and Bell Green at the north-east – offered a new start (Fig 77). Fortuitously, the new suburbs were near established wartime 'shadow' engineering factories, now regarded as permanent, 'clean' neighbours, so that local employment was guaranteed and commuting distances convenient even for residents that did not yet own cars. The suburbs fitted Lewis Mumford's theory of the 'poly-nucleated city' and Patrick Abercrombie's ideas, reiterated in the Ministry of Health's *Housing Manual* of 1944,[86] of the 'neighbourhood unit'. This was a self-contained community surrounded by parks and woodland and composed of 'neighbourhood groups',

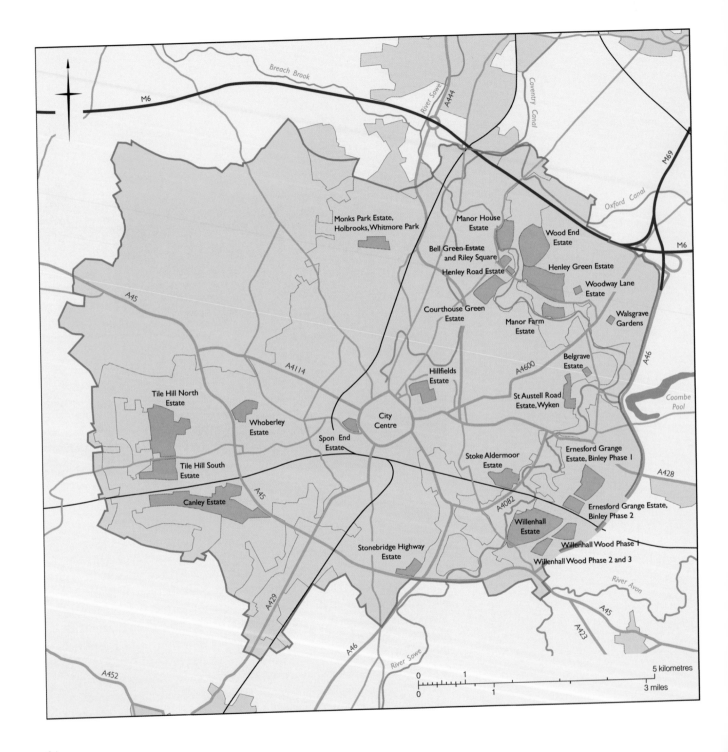

Breach Brook

M6

River Sowe

A444

Coventry Canal

Oxford Canal

M69

M6

Monks Park Estate,
Holbrooks, Whitmore Park

Manor House
Estate

Wood End
Estate

Bell Green Estate
and Riley Square

Henley Green Estate

Henley Road Estate

Woodway Lane
Estate

A45

Courthouse Green
Estate

Manor Farm
Estate

Walsgrave
Gardens

A46

A4114

A4600

Belgrave
Estate

Coombe
Pool

Hillfields
Estate

Tile Hill North
Estate

St Austell Road
Estate, Wyken

Whoberley
Estate

City
Centre

Spon End
Estate

Stoke Aldermoor
Estate

Ernesford Grange
Estate, Binley Phase 1

A428

Tile Hill South
Estate

A45

Ernesford Grange Estate,
Binley Phase 2

Canley Estate

A4082

Willenhall
Estate

Willenhall Wood Phase 1

Stonebridge Highway
Estate

Willenhall Wood Phase 2 and 3

River Avon

A429

A46

River Sowe

A45

A423

A452

A42S

0   1   5 kilometres

0   1   3 miles

Figure 77 (opposite)
Location of the post-war estates (coloured pink).

based around elementary (primary) schools, with a 'neighbourhood centre' at its heart consisting of a church, library, shops and other community buildings. The mayor, J C Lee Gordon, explained in 1946:

> The suburbs have generally developed as an unplanned growth. In order to develop a social sense it is very necessary to divide the suburbs into definite zones, each with its own identity, and each with a social centre, or focal point, at which group activities may be carried on which are wider than the activities of a small family group.[87]

It was easy for Gibson to define the type of housing layout he did not want – it was the endless streets of semi-detached houses of Radford – but finding a new form which encompassed both the esoteric 'new urban order', described by Mumford in *The Culture of Cities*, and the practicalities of the *Housing Manual* which defined floor areas and standard plans for post-war housing, proved rather more difficult. However, at the Monks Park estate (1946–8), at Holbrooks in the north of the city, he introduced a mixture of house types set in short terraces around 'village greens' with sites reserved for a playground and nursery school (Fig 78). The whole layout was contrived to be almost symmetrical about the three major greens, like some grand Beaux-Arts plan, except for a curved road (Everdon Road) winding informally through the grids. The arrangement was reminiscent of the new villages described by Thomas Sharp in his *The Anatomy of the Village*, a best-selling Penguin paperback of 1946. In addition, the idea of a suburb composed of a series of greens surrounded by housing had

Figure 78 (right)
Monks Park estate, Holbrooks (Donald Gibson,
city architect, 1946–8).
[DP164857]

been proposed by Charles Reilly, the former professor of Architecture at Liverpool University, for a new suburb of Birkenhead, published as *The Reilly Plan – a new way of life* in 1945. Many of Reilly's greens were oval and Sharp warned that

> A complicated pattern of elaborate and artificial circular shapes would be completely destructive of the directness and simplicity which should characterise the plan-arrangements in a village. The square, the quadrangle and the close are the most useful plan-shapes for modern conditions of living; ... These shapes, either singly or in combination, are capable of a great deal of diversity.[88]

All of the estates built under Gibson's control – Tile Hill South (750 dwellings), Tile Hill North (1,928), Willenhall (1,276), Courthouse Green (556) and Wood End (1,804), Henley Green (1,268) and Manor House (451) (which together made up the Bell Green Estate) – were conceived as a series of rectilinear village greens of different sizes, enclosed by housing on three or four sides. Generally, the layouts followed the 1949 *Housing Manual* which had included Monks Park as an example. Sometimes, as at Monks Park, the greens were symmetrically arranged but, more usually, the arrangements were informal and greens of different sizes formed a changing sequence of spaces across the estates. Initially, two-storey terraced and semi-detached houses were arranged in conventional perimeter blocks enclosing back gardens, occasionally with 'banjo' cul-de-sacs – forms of planning familiar from inter-war estates like Becontree and Welwyn Garden City. Later, longer uninterrupted terraces were introduced, as at Willenhall and Henley Green, and the architecture became more striking. The greatest set piece was the block of flats, Jardine Crescent, which curved around the main green at Tile Hill (Fig 79), reflecting Sharp's dictum that 'a subtle curve echoing some natural line, like that of a stream or of a hillside, may provide a very telling foil against the common rectangular forms'.[89] When the same form was tried as a series of straight blocks against the curving Wappenbury Road, Wood End, the effect was diminished. The greens and housing worked best when they were laid out on an approximate north–south, east–west grid, as at Tile Hill, Willenhall, Henley Green and Manor House. Where, like the groups off Lapworth Road and Milverton Road, Wood End,

Figure 79
Jardine Crescent, Tile Hill (Donald Gibson, city architect and planning officer, c 1950–2). [DP164762]

the roads and housing groups too closely followed the contours, the resulting amorphous spaces and convoluted circulation only confused, the effect exaggerated by the preponderance of tightly packed, two-storey terraces. Generally though, the house types were varied within the estates in order to promote a mixed community, the overall mix of housing being interpreted from the waiting list statistics. This resulted in a high proportion of flats for single people and young families. The flats came in many forms: some, like the three- and four-storey *zeilenbau* blocks and the two-storey corner blocks with outside staircases, followed the *Housing Manual* plans. Jardine Crescent uniquely incorporated two-storey maisonettes above ground-floor flats, but the most common form was a plain, four-storey flat-roofed square block (Fig 80).

Coventry pioneered three- and four-storey 'T'-shaped pitched roof blocks with three flats per floor and, at Tile Hill, adjacent to the neighbourhood centre, Gibson designed three 11-storey 'point block' versions (1950–3)[90] with a 'skip stop' lift serving the third, sixth and ninth floors only (Fig 81). Their inspiration, though not their exact plans, came from published Swedish prototypes and Nikolaus Pevsner noted that Tile Hill gave 'a vertical accent lacking in the other [estates] of the same years. The blocks themselves are far from distinguished, but their role in the visual play is most important'.[91]

After their success at Stonebridge Highway estate, Wimpey's became the City's preferred housing contractor, using the 'no fines' system for Tile Hill North, Stoke Aldermoor (965 dwellings), Willenhall and Wood End and many other smaller developments. The grey rendered walls and concrete tiled roofs were repeated across the city and Jardine Crescent was named for their site foreman, Dan Jardine. The traditionally built Tile Hill South was in red brick and brick was also used to add some variety to the 'no fines' estates as well as at Manor House. Of necessity, the detailing was austere but some decoration was added with panels of coloured tiles at the entrances to the flats, balustrades of Festival ironwork and perforated painted metal (Fig 82), and lattice timber screens to the porches of the old people's bungalows (Fig 83). Exceptionally, the long three-storey flats at Henley Green had alternating panels of yellow brick

Figure 80 (above, left)
Flats, Violet Close, Manor House estate (Donald Gibson, city architect and planning officer, c 1950–4. The most common of Coventry's standard types which was repeated at Tile Hill, Wood End, Willenhall and Henley Green.
[DP164841]

Figure 81 (above)
Point block flats, Ferrers Close, Tile Hill (Donald Gibson, city architect and planning officer, 1950–3).
[DP164774]

Figure 82 (above)
Detail of entrance and balconies to flats, Stonebridge Highway estate (Donald Gibson, city architect and planning officer, 1950–1). A range of coloured tiles, paint colours and balcony balustrades differentiated the entrances.
[DP164785]

Figure 83 (above, right)
Old people's housing, Delius Street, Tile Hill (Donald Gibson, city architect and planning officer, c 1950–3).
[DP164772]

and coloured render with the balconies framed out in reconstructed stone with diamond-pattern metal balustrades. The landscape too was austere. Although all the houses had back gardens big enough for the growing of vegetables, the fronts and greens were unadorned open lawns and very few new trees were added. The flats were often marooned in open grass with no private space except for an occasional drying green and row of stores off a parking yard. When the houses and flats were lucky enough to inherit old trees, however, the effect was miraculously different, taking on the appearance of a real village green or even the idyllic landscapes illustrated in G E Kidder Smith's *Sweden Builds* of 1950 or Bertil Hultén's popular Penguin paperback *Building Modern Sweden* of 1951, both aspirational references for young architects (Fig 84). The beautiful parkland dividing the neighbourhoods, like the valley between Wood End and Manor House (Fig 85) or the Sowe valley west of Willenhall, compensated somewhat for the baldness of the internal landscape. Existing woodlands adjacent to all of the estates were carefully preserved and the 70-acre (28.3ha) Tile Hill Wood, to the west of the housing, was declared a site of special scientific interest in 1952.

Figure 84
Wimpey 'no fines' housing, Dunhill Avenue and
Dyson Street, Tile Hill (Donald Gibson, city architect
and planning officer, c 1950–2).
[DP164769]

Figure 85
Housing, Almond Tree Avenue, Manor House estate
(Donald Gibson, city architect and planning officer,
c 1950–4. The houses look out across the valley of
the River Sowe towards Wood End.
[DP164843]

Accommodating the car – Willenhall Wood and the later estates

The early estates took little account of the private motor car. Cars were parked on the streets and the few lock-up garages were rented separately from the houses. The 1949 *Housing Manual* hardly mentioned cars, but the 1953 supplement introduced the 'service cul-de-sac' layout with the example of Radburn, New Jersey (from 1929), the pioneering American planned community, where independent footpath and road systems served housing from peripheral roads thereby providing safe, vehicle-free access to the houses and to amenities like shops and schools. The idea was strongly advocated by Mumford but, despite the exponential increase of car ownership, it did not appear in Coventry until Ling's Willenhall Wood estate of 650 dwellings (1958–9).[92] It was the first large-scale Radburn-type planning layout in Britain[93] but built at about twice the density of its American cousin. The peripheral road, Middle Ride, led to a series of cul-de-sacs within tight courtyards of housing where they served parking, some garages and back entrances to the houses through small gardens. At the front of the houses, the familiar greenways and village greens led through the whole estate and to the nursery school, shops and public house without crossing a road (Fig 86).

Figure 86
Greenspace between Wimpey 'no fines' houses in Leyside and Jamescroft, Willenhall Wood estate Phase 1 (Arthur Ling, city architect and planning officer, 1958–9).
[DP164791]

Thereafter, all of Coventry's public housing was laid out on Radburn principles but, as the demand for parking space and garages grew, the areas of public space and private gardens shrank in order to preserve the density on what was becoming increasingly scarce land. At the later phases of Willenhall Wood, built south of Middle Ride (1960, 217 dwellings and between 1962 and 1965, 312 dwellings; Fig 87) and the Ernesford Grange estate Phase III at Binley, south of Quorn Way, (c 1965–9) long ribbons of houses enclosed featureless courtyards of cars, far bigger in area than the public green spaces. However, the best of these at Ernesford Grange was still large enough to take on the character of a village green with big trees and ample space for informal games (Fig 88). The Woodway Lane estate at Henley Green (1962–4, altered) designed for the Midlands Housing Consortium by Fred Lloyd Roche after he left Ling's department, was the first to realise the architectural implications of each house having a garage, an imperative of the 1961 Parker Morris report *Homes for Today and Tomorrow*. A dense matrix of 133 narrow two-storey pitched-roof houses with attached garages, cul-de-sac roads and interlinking, narrow green spaces evenly covered the whole site (Fig 89). The houses drew consistent praise from the architectural press for their design and economy.

Figure 87
Greenspace between traditionally built red-brick houses in Weymouth Close and Cardiff Close, Willenhall Wood estate Phase III (Arthur Ling, city architect and planning officer, 1962–5).
[DP164795]

Figure 88
'Village green' on the Ernesford Grange estate Phase III
(Arthur Ling, city architect and planning officer,
c 1965–9).
[DP164805]

Figure 89
Woodway Lane estate, Henley Green (Fred Lloyd
Roche, 1962–4). Vehicular access to garage
courtyards from Woodway Lane, foreground,
and Pandora Road, top left.
[29205_048]

The tenants criticised the poor soundproofing, lack of storage, tiny gardens and inadequate heating but their children were happy playing on the roads leaving the traffic-free greens almost unused.[94]

Woodway Lane set a trend for dense, mono-typical housing. At the Manor Farm estate (1964–7, altered),[95] south of Henley Road, Bell Green, a series of long cul-de-sacs from the perimeter road, Hermes Crescent, led to parking courtyards and garages within groups of flat-roofed houses (now altered) (*see* p 80). The groups were separated by narrow footpaths in green strips which led to a large central park, the overall effect somewhat like the original Radburn. However, for smaller estates, it was efficient to leave cars parked at the perimeters and access the houses by foot. The Henley Road estate (1967–70, 80 dwellings),[96] adjacent to the Bell Green neighbourhood centre, achieved this from two cul-de-sacs and most of the houses looked inwards into three peaceful garden squares (Fig 90). At Walsgrave Gardens, Walsgrave (1968–9, 94 dwellings, altered) by Thorne Barton & Tulip for the Coventry and Midlands Housing Association, flat-roofed 'cluster' houses were grouped in pairs and fours around internal patios. Cars were parked on the streets and in perimeter garages and access to the houses was by narrow kasbah-like alleyways with no common green space at all (Fig 91).

Figure 90
Benedict Square, Henley Road estate, Bell Green (Terence Gregory, city architect and planning officer, 1967–70).
[DP164837]

Figure 91
Pedestrian alleyway, Walsgrave Gardens,
Walsgrave (Thorne Barton & Tulip, 1968–9).
[DP164809]

Except for Walsgrave Gardens, all the later estates, including Willenhall Wood, contained flats in blocks. Ling and Gregory added new types to the repertoire: Ling designed a two-storey pyramid-roofed block for Yarningdale Road, Willenhall and Gregory a more interesting four-storey, square block with a flat roof and a mono-pitched skylight to a central common stair.[97] Both were clad in brickwork, Gregory's with distinctive precast concrete 'saddlebag' balconies hanging from the façades. Four examples appeared at Bredon Avenue, Ernesford Grange, one at Henley Road and four south of Hermes Crescent, Manor Farm (two now demolished), with their own pedestrian underpass (now demolished) under Hermes Crescent in true Radburn manner (Fig 92).

The Woodway Lane houses had innovative aluminium sash windows and were clad with white boarding and grey asbestos tiles and these materials were repeated on similar houses along Bredon Avenue, Ernesford Grange Phase 1 (designed with Diamond Redfern & Partners) in various pastel colours. They looked and proved insubstantial and the final phase of Ernesford Grange, south of Quorn Way, and all the later estates used brick and traditional construction. The last 'no fines' was phase two of Willenhall Wood and there were only two further examples of system building. Manor Farm used 'Hallamshire'

Figure 92
Corinthian Place flats, Manor Farm estate, Hermes
Road, Bell Green (Terence Gregory, city architect
and planning officer, 1964–7).
[DP164855]

prefabricated timber framing, built by Vic Hallam of Langley Mill, Derbyshire, a firm which had made its name making prefabricated school classrooms. The two-storey houses were clad in painted timber boarding and fragile 'mathematical' tiles (imitating brickwork) and the single-storey houses were clad in buff bricks. Calder Homes of Washington built three terraces of two-storey 'large box' houses, designed by Harding & Horsman, at 397–429 Tile Hill Lane (1964–5, 17 houses), in totally prefabricated units delivered by lorry so that four boxes made one house. The experiments were not repeated.

Neighbourhood centres – shops, churches and community buildings

A fundamental principle of the neighbourhood unit was the focus of the new communities on the neighbourhood centres. Inevitably, the building of these followed the housing and the late or non-delivery of the facilities promised was a constant source of conflict between the City and the new residents. To better understand the sociological implications of the planning and design of the neighbourhood centres, the City commissioned a sociological survey of existing estates, the first of its kind, from Philip Sargant Florence, professor of Commerce at Birmingham University, who reported from 1950 to 1954. Unsurprisingly, the report identified the cinema, the church, libraries, public houses, social clubs and community centres and shopping as the principal activities of the communities and examined their patterns of use, but drew no conclusions on how the statistics would affect physical planning. Interpretation was left to Gibson and Ling's staff, in particular to the planner, Wilfred Burns (1923–84), at Coventry from 1949 to 1958, who expounded his theories in his *British Shopping Centres* of 1959.[98] The model for the neighbourhood centre was the village and the various community buildings were loosely arranged around or near the greens. The small greens at Wood End and Willenhall both had shopping precincts, the former a single-storey 'L'-shape and the latter a much more sophisticated 'U'-shaped pedestrianised plaza surrounded by shops with brick three-storey flats above (both now demolished). The 27 shops at Tile Hill (1951–5, altered)[99] were built along Jardine Crescent away from the green opposite Limbrick Wood, presumably attempting to serve both the new estate and the inter-war houses at Lime Tree Park to the east (Fig 93). An arcade of shops followed the street and opened into a central square and squares at the east and west ends; above, four blocks of ten 'duplex' flats (served from a single corridor on the second floor), clad in black and light-grey Vitrolite and buff brick, ran at right angles to the street and faced the squares.

Figure 93
Neighbourhood centre shops and flats, Jardine Crescent, Tile Hill (Donald Gibson, city architect and planning officer, 1951–5). The original cladding was grey and black Vitrolite glass with a few panels of brightly coloured Vitroslab.
[DP164775]

In addition to these examples and the small parades of shops at Henley Green and Willenhall Wood, Burns also advocated isolated 'corner' shops, conveniently placed throughout a neighbourhood, together with a few much larger neighbourhood centres of 100 to 150 shops each – like the established centre at Jubilee Crescent, Radford, one of Sargant Florence's survey areas. The Bell Green District Centre, Riley Square (1957–65)[100] was the only example built (Fig 94). An immense pedestrian plaza stretching from Henley Road to Roseberry Avenue was surrounded by shops and a supermarket. At its centre, raised above more shops, was the 17-storey tower, Dewis House, with four long blocks of four-storey flats surrounding it, arranged in a pinwheel pattern (the block on Henley Road remained unfinished) and raised on pilotis to make entrances to the plaza. Its scale was greater than the Lower Precinct and rivalled the size of the centres of the new towns, like Stevenage and Harlow. *New Coventry Architecture* heralded Riley Square as 'a notable popular success, with bustling crowds for most of the day, and [it] integrates social and commercial interests in the neighbourhood'.[101]

Figure 94
Bell Green District Centre, Riley Square, Bell Green (Arthur Ling, city architect and planning officer, 1957–65). Four-storey flats raised on pilotis surround the pedestrianised shopping precinct with Dewis House in the middle.
[DP164833]

Riley Square and the Willenhall precinct contained public libraries[102] but it was not until 1968 that the branch library arrived in Tile Hill (now demolished and replaced) to complete the set of community buildings on the green, including a clinic, social club, community centre, the Black Prince public house (by W S Hattrell & Partners who also designed the Winnall, Willenhall, both 1958) and two churches – the modest brick Baptist Church by J Roland Sidwell and Basil Spence's St Oswald (1954–7). St Oswald, together with St John the Divine, Willenhall (Fig 95) and St Chad, Wood End (all listed Grade II), was commissioned by Bishop Gorton during the building of the Cathedral. Spence ingeniously designed standard elements of church, church hall and free-standing bell tower which could be arranged to fit the different sites, each built by Wimpey's in conjunction with their housing contracts. Standard brick vicarages were added by 1961. The bell tower was an open concrete frame with timber slats and coloured metal louvres, the hall a simple monopitch roofed rectangular box and the church a tall, single volume formed of precast concrete portal frames infilled with thick 'no fines' concrete. The shallow pitched roof of the church was decorated with coloured fibreboard panels but otherwise the interior was unadorned, dramatic effect provided by light from the windows to the altar and nave, the arrangement slightly different in each church (Fig 96).

Figure 95
St John the Divine, Robin Hood Road, Willenhall
(Basil Spence & Partners, 1954–7).
[DP031201]

Figure 96
*Nave of St Oswald, Jardine Crescent, Tile Hill
(Basil Spence & Partners, 1954–7). The wall
hanging behind the altar of St Aidan and St Oswald
is by Gerald Holtom.*
[DP031223]

Spence's three churches were paid for by war reparation grants from a single bombed inner city church but, when more money was available, new churches adopted the contemporary decorative style established by the Festival of Britain. Christchurch, Cheylesmore (1953–8, now listed Grade II) by A H Gardner & Partners and St Nicholas, Coundon (1954–7, derelict) by Lavender Twentyman & Percy were 'reparation' churches (Christchurch replacing its namesake in the city centre), both remarkable for the richness and colour of their interiors and the eccentricity of their exterior forms. St Nicholas was the more restrained: the exterior of sloping brickwork walls, curved copper roof and tapering campanile (Fig 97); the interior panelled, diamond-pattern in walnut and mahogany, floors of Hornton stone and Westmorland slate beneath a sky-blue ceiling. Christchurch balanced a squat brick bell tower with full-height windows expressing the three equal bays of a nave formed from shallow concrete vaults. The interior was a collage of timber panelling, white chequerboard ceiling panels, purple and crimson plaster, raw brickwork and bird-cage pendant lights (Fig 98). It was described by the *Architects' Journal* as 'Pleasure Gardens

Figure 97
St Nicholas, Sherwood Jones Close, Coundon; derelict
in 2014 (Lavender Twentyman & Percy, 1954–7).
[DP164860]

Figure 98
Altar and nave of Christchurch, Frankpledge Road,
Cheylesmore (A H Gardner & Partners, 1953–8).
[DP173112]

Figure 99
Nave of St Francis of Assisi, Links Road, Radford
(N F Cachemaille-Day, 1957–9).
[DP164858]

pastiche'[103] but may be seen now as one of the great church interiors of the 1950s. Even the more humble churches could be decorated. St Francis of Assisi, Radford (1957–9) by N F Cachemaille-Day of London, a prolific church architect who designed five churches in Coventry, was a conventional aisled church of plain yellow brick but the altar was covered by a startling blue-domed, gold-columned ciborium (Fig 99). As with the Cathedral, the altars of the new Coventry churches, unaffected by the ecumenical movement which advocated centralised worship, remained traditionally placed beyond the congregation. This was due to conservative diocesan committees rather than to Bishop Gorton himself, and it is fitting that the only centralised church was Bishop Gorton's Memorial Church (St Christopher) at Allesley Park designed by Cachemaille-Day (1959–60) in the form of a Greek cross.[104]

In the absence of facilities provided by the City, the church halls offered a focus for the communities especially in the provision of temporary maternity and child welfare clinics. Although the pre-war swimming bath at Foleshill was extended (1960–2, by City Architect's Department), the decision to build the Central Swimming Baths ruled out the building of further neighbourhood pools. No developer was willing to risk a new suburban cinema. Only the pre-war Godiva at Tile Hill, adjacent to the Fletchhampstead Highway, served a new suburb, but the refurbishment in 1965 by G R Stone reduced the seating from 1,350 to 500 and it closed in 1976. Most successful and popular were the neighbourhood social clubs, established at Willenhall, Bell Green (within Riley Square) and Tile Hill by the 1960s, in addition to those run by the larger factories, like Standard-Triumph at Canley and Massey Ferguson at Tile Hill. At its height in the late 1960s, Tile Hill Social Club designed by K R B McKnight (1962 and 1966, now demolished) was one of the largest in the city with 1,350 members, a concert hall for 350 and activities such as boxing, a film club and Saturday morning discos for children.

Neighbourhood centres – education and schools

The blitz destroyed five Coventry schools (equivalent to about 4,000 school places) and a further 20 needed replacement, but it was the post-war birth rate that created the urgent need for new schools. The city's primary school population was about 20,000 in 1946, over 25,000 in 1951 and 28,000 in 1960. The secondary school population doubled to over 12,000 from 1946 to 1951, augmented by the raising of the school leaving age to 15, and increased to over 21,000 by 1960. The Butler Education Act of 1944 introduced universal secondary education but made no mention of comprehensive schools, then beginning to find favour with the most progressive teachers. The ideology was enthusiastically embraced by the Coventry Education Committee, although, try as it might, the four established grammar schools were not abolished. Coventry divided primary schools into nursery, infants and junior stages, usually in connected buildings. Secondary schools were organised into 'houses' of about 150 pupils each, intended to instil a sense of community life, each school made up of five pairs of houses. Primary schools were placed at the centre of neighbourhood groups, within walking distance of their catchment areas. Secondary schools were located as evenly as possible across the city and on exceptionally large sites of 30 acres (12.1ha) or more to allow for low-density buildings and space for gardens, playing fields and expansion.

The school building programme, especially the primary schools, could not be delayed and Gibson, busy with the city centre and housing and already experiencing problems with traditional construction, turned once again to prefabricated buildings. His friend and former deputy at the Isle of Ely and pupil from Liverpool, Stirrat Johnson-Marshall, Percy Johnson-Marshall's brother, was deputy county architect at Hertfordshire where he was pioneering schools built of lightweight steel frames and precast concrete cladding. With knowledge of these, Gibson and his school's section architect, William Glare, developed their own system with the engineer F W Lister Heathcote of Brockhouse & Co, who had collaborated on the prototype GBS house and who happened to be a pupil of Gibson's father from Manchester University.[105] The schools were planned on the 8ft 3in (2.5m) structural grid used by Hertfordshire and recommended by the Ministry of Education in the late 1940s. The first three prototypes were the Sir Henry Parkes Primary, Canley (demolished), Manor Park Primary, Cheylesmore and Radford Primary, Coundon, all built from 1946 to 1947. All were combined nursery, infant and junior schools with similar 'finger' plans of classrooms served by long corridors stretching from central, double-height assembly halls. The utilitarian rendered concrete block walls, flat roofs, steel-framed windows and brick water towers were somewhat ameliorated by each classroom opening into its own courtyard with paving, lawns and trees, giving both privacy and acoustic separation.[106] Gibson and the newly appointed director of education, Walter Chinn, no doubt thought that the City could do better and appointed three firms of young architects – Arcon, whose partner Edric Neel had worked with Gibson on the Radiation house and had designed the very successful Arcon 'prefab' bungalow, the Architects' Co-partnership (ACP) and Richard Sheppard & Partners, both of whom had worked on schools for Hertfordshire. Arcon and ACP used the Hertfordshire version of the steel frame, produced by Hills of West Bromwich, and introduced to Coventry a staggered plan arrangement of classrooms first seen at Templewood School in Hertfordshire in 1950. This reduced the apparent corridor lengths and scale of the exterior, expressing the classrooms as almost separate 'pavilions' with fully glazed fronts incorporating brightly coloured panels. The form was used at ACP's Richard Lee Primary, Wyken (1952, 1957, demolished; Fig 100) on a difficult, sloping site and, more comfortably, at their Wyken Croft Primary (1952, demolished; Fig 101). These were clad in horizontal concrete planks but Arcon's Alderman's Green Primary (1953, demolished) was clad in brick with a first-floor staff block connecting the infants and junior sections across an open loggia that separated the entrance courtyard from the playing fields, proving that the grid frame was not restrictive and could be imaginatively and stylishly interpreted.

Figure 100
Classroom wing, Richard Lee Primary School,
The Drive, Wyken (Architects' Co-partnership, 1952).
[DP164815]

Figure 101
Classroom wing, Wyken Croft Primary School,
Wyken Croft, Wyken (Architects' Co-partnership, 1952).
[DP164831]

Richard Sheppard was architectural advisor to the Bristol Aeroplane Company (BAC) who had devised a building system made from aluminium components, an idea that Gibson had been anxious to prove since 1940. The prototype Coventry school, Whitmore Park Primary (1949–51, demolished), was a strictly gridded multiple-'H'- shaped plan with all the classrooms facing south-east and served by long corridors. The gable ends and concrete framed halls were clad in brick but, otherwise, all the components of structure, fenestration and cladding were in painted aluminium, the facades braced with triangular aluminium box mullions (Fig 102). Although the system was innovative, the problem was the long corridors which Stirrat Johnson-Marshall, who became director of the Development Group of the Ministry of Education in 1948, likened to a prison.[107] In 1950, the Ministry announced revised cost limits for schools, implying significant reductions in floor area and radical revisions to standard corridor plans like Whitmore Park. Gibson, quick to exploit an opportunity, agreed to develop the BAC system with the Ministry and get further prototypes of primary and secondary schools built to the new cost limits as part of the City's programme. The first was Limbrick Wood Primary at Tile Hill (1950–2, now listed Grade II; Fig 103) built as two separate schools for juniors and infants.[108] Classrooms were in pairs served through short lobbies directly

Figure 102
Façade of the junior dining room, Whitmore Park Primary School, Halford Lane, Whitmore Park (Richard Sheppard & Partners, 1949–51).
[© the authors]

Figure 103
Limbrick Wood Primary School, Bush Close, Tile Hill
(Development Group of the Ministry of Education and
Donald Gibson, city architect and planning officer,
1950–2).
[DP162203]

from the central hall, a dining area opened off it and corridors were almost completely eliminated. Compared to previous schools, the area per place was reduced by 6.4 per cent; the usable area increased by 18.5 per cent and the classrooms 65 per cent bigger. It was a quiet revolution that was to affect British primary school planning for the next 20 years.

The new secondary schools

Although the sites were big, secondary schools needed to be multi-storey to avoid excessive spread. Coventry's first attempt to find an architectural expression for the 'house' idea resulted in Glare's Caludon Castle, Wyken (1951–5, demolished), using a Brockhouse steel frame, where five paired houses in two-storey 'T'-shapes ranged along the contour in front of separate sports, teaching and administration blocks. The walking distances were immense. With the next three comprehensive schools – Woodlands, Tile Hill (1953–7, now listed Grade II), Lyng Hall, Wyken (1953–5, demolished) and Whitley Abbey, Whitley (1955–6, demolished) – Coventry invented new forms which rank them among the best contemporary schools in the country. Woodlands and Lyng Hall were designed by the Ministry of Education under Johnson-Marshall and Whitley Abbey by John Barker,[109] Glare's successor, under Gibson and Ling. Woodlands was built on a Hills steel frame with concrete plank cladding; Lyng Hall and Whitley Abbey used the BAC MkII system, adapted for use up to three floors with a steel frame, and clad with fluted aluminium panels on a 4ft (1.2m) module, the frame and floor beams clearly expressed externally in darker

cladding. The planning principle – best demonstrated at Woodlands – was to
divide the functions into separate buildings, closely spaced on an irregular
rectilinear grid like a mini-campus, forming a chequerboard of buildings and
open courtyards (Fig 104). Footpaths winding through the courtyards connected
the buildings and led to the sports pitches on the south. Although the
architecture was plain and unadorned, the juxtaposition of different sized blocks
and the rich landscape of lawns, trees and shrubs made for special and
distinctive places. At Lyng Hall, the site of an old farm, fewer, somewhat bigger
blocks were set around a large, central courtyard, carefully retaining old trees
and hedges. The existing pitched-roof farm buildings were converted for an art
and craft block enclosing the old farmyard and forming a school garden as part
of the sequence of open spaces. The most idyllic was Whitley Abbey, built within
a mature 19th-century landscape of wellingtonias and beech trees and set
around a lake with a slim concrete bridge linking the administration block
(containing two halls, library and staffrooms) to the houses (Fig 105).

When Gibson left Coventry for Nottinghamshire in 1955, he took his ideas
of prefabrication with him. Nottinghamshire too had a crisis with schools and,
together with a group of architects formerly at Hertfordshire, Gibson invented a

Figure 104 (left)
Woodlands School, Broad Lane, Tile Hill (Development
Group of the Ministry of Education and Donald Gibson,
city architect and planning officer, 1953–7).
[BB95/11074-80]

Figure 105 (opposite)
Whitley Abbey School, Abbey Road, Whitley
photographed by Eric de Maré (Arthur Ling,
city architect and planning officer, 1955–6).
[AA98/06083]

new system of prefabrication using the Brockhouse steel frame and pad foundations similar to those of the Radiation house. It was especially designed for areas subject to mining subsidence. The new system was ready within a year but, needing bulk contracts to make it economic, Gibson hastily signed up neighbouring Derbyshire and Coventry to form a consortium, eventually to become CLASP (Consortium of Local Authorities Special Programme) with a total of seven local authorities. From 1957, most of Coventry's new schools – primary and secondary – were built in CLASP, replacing the other systems, although a few schools like ACP's Alderman's Green Primary, a precursor of the CLASP plan form, and St Michael's Church of England Primary, Cheylesmore (1958–9, demolished) were traditionally constructed in brick. Apart from the speed of construction, one of the advantages of CLASP was that the designer could use a variety of external materials. The delightful Ernesford Grange Primary, Binley, for example, used vertical concrete planks for the infants section and handsome green aggregate panels for the juniors as well as brightly coloured panels in the classroom windows (Fig 106). Like Limbrick Wood, Ernesford Grange was a typical CLASP plan with the classrooms in clusters, but tightly packed around the central hall, the junior school with an internal courtyard.

Figure 106
Ernesford Grange Primary School, Foxton Road, Binley (Arthur Ling, city architect and planning officer, c 1960).
[© the authors]

CLASP was at its best for small primary schools. When used for larger buildings, for example at Henley College of Further Education, Henley Green (1962–4, altered) or Binley Park Comprehensive School (1957–9 and 1960–2, demolished), both in mining subsidence areas and up to four storeys high, it became more formulaic and repetitive. However, it was used at both Lyng Hall and Whitley Abbey after the BAC system was discontinued in 1955, demonstrating yet another advantage of the 'campus' school plan – that it could be extended easily. CLASP was constantly developed. The Mark III and IV versions used white precast concrete panel cladding as used on Gregory's President Kennedy School, Whitmore Park (1965–7 and 1973, altered; Fig 107). The five separate two-storey house blocks were in a staggered row against the playing fields and the strictly gridded plan, arranged around five courtyards, lined up behind. A particular feature was the circular music block sitting in a pond with fountains – the overall effect reminiscent of a miniature university which, perhaps, is no coincidence for the contemporary York and Bath universities were built in a similar CLASP system.

Figure 107
President Kennedy School, Rookery Lane, Whitmore Park. (Terence Gregory, city architect and planning officer, 1965–7 and 1973).
[DP172649]

Figure 108
Belgrave estate, Westmorland Road, Wyken (Arthur Ling, city architect and planning officer, 1959–62). [DP164824]

By 1970, Coventry had built 11 new comprehensive schools and over 50 new primary schools, serving over 80 percent of the city's primary school population. Nearly 27,000 families lived in city-owned housing, mostly in new suburbs. Through the 1950s, the City built over 1,000 dwellings per year, peaking in 1957 at almost 2,000. However, private house builders, released from the licensing system in 1954, managed to build 13,000 houses from 1946 to 1960 (as against the City's 14,000) and, by the beginning of the 1960s, were achieving over 1,500 houses per year although this declined significantly by the end of the decade.[110] Even the Housing Committee tried private housing, building for sale the red-brick Belgrave Estate, Wyken (1959–62) using the City's direct works labour (Fig 108). The experiment made a loss of £15,000 and was not repeated. In 1967, the new Conservative administration introduced severe and unpopular rent increases (only to have them curtailed by the Labour Government's Prices and Incomes Board), disbanded the City's direct works organisation for private enterprise, replaced the Policy Advisory Committee for a centralised Policy Committee and introduced a scheme for tenants to buy their houses with council mortgages.[111] By 1969, 1,000 council houses had been sold and, although building contracts already placed continued to the mid-1970s, the sale signalled the end of council housing and Hodgkinson's 'socialist city'.

7

The status and influence of Coventry

Many British cities – Southampton, Plymouth, Hull, Canterbury, Bristol and Exeter – were bombed and suffered damage equal to or greater than Coventry. Their post-war rebuilding followed the same bureaucratic processes and each of them developed a post-war plan formulated by a consultant planner, for example by Abercrombie at Plymouth and Hull and Sharp at Exeter, or by the authority itself. The scope and ambition of these plans varied enormously but, by the late 1940s, most of them had pragmatically elected to adapt their pre-war layouts with guidance from the MTCP's *The Redevelopment of Central Areas* so that functional zoning, the introduction of ring roads and the clearance and rebuilding of specific small areas typified them all (Fig 109). Mostly these plans avoided grand gestures – Abercrombie's Beaux-Arts plan for Hull was rejected for something more affordable and deliverable, Sharp's Princesshay in Exeter, the first pedestrianised shopping street in Britain in 1949, hardly affected the existing city centre plan and Bristol's Broadmead shopping precinct widened existing trafficked streets and introduced just one new circus, based on Georgian Bath. The exception was Abercrombie's plan for Plymouth (Fig 110) which wholly rebuilt the entire city centre unencumbered by old buildings, introducing a grand Beaux-Arts axis from the railway station to the sea with precisely zoned new streets set about it on a rectilinear grid.[112] Once adopted in 1946, very much ahead of Coventry, the plan was never materially revised so that Plymouth can claim to be the city of the welfare state. The architecture of Plymouth's city centre was produced by developers and their architects and, in common with most cities, the architect's department was involved with development control and planning only in the city centres and with new housing, schools and community buildings in the suburbs. Few of these departments regarded themselves as pioneers; rather than leaders or innovators, they were followers of new ideas held in common and few cities – Plymouth again an exception – had the visionary political leadership of Coventry.

From the beginning Coventry had a special status. It was the first British provincial city to be blitzed and its cathedral the only British cathedral to be destroyed by the war. King George VI and the Home Secretary, Herbert Morrison, visited two days after 14 November 1940, sent by a government uncertain of local morale. The king and queen visited in February 1942 to see and approve of Gibson's plans for rebuilding and again in April 1951 to see the completed Broadgate garden and the construction of Broadgate

'Coventry Rebuilds', front cover of Architectural Design *December 1958 designed by Theo Crosby to symbolise the destruction and reconstruction of Coventry. [Reproduced with permission of John Wiley & Sons; © Dido Crosby; the Theo Crosby archive is now held in Brighton]*

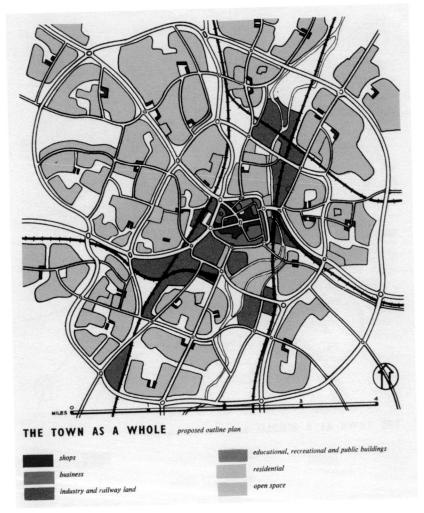

THE TOWN AS A WHOLE *proposed outline plan*

▮ shops

▮ business

▮ industry and railway land

▮ educational, recreational and public buildings

▮ residential

▮ open space

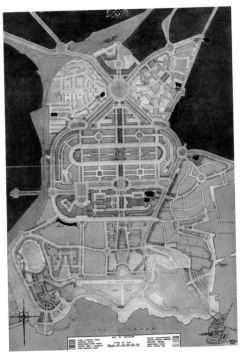

Figure 109 (left)
'The town as a whole' from The Redevelopment of
Central Areas, *1947. The ideal reordering of an old
city into functional precincts with public buildings,
shops and businesses in the centre and housing
arranged into neighbourhoods on the periphery.*
*[Ministry of Town and Country Planning 1947, 19;
© HMSO]*

Figure 110 (above)
*The Plan for Plymouth, 1943 (Patrick Abercrombie
and James Paton Watson, city engineer and surveyor).*
*[Abercrombie, P and Paton Watson, J 1943, 66;
reproduced by permission of the Plymouth and
West Devon Record Office, ref 1655; © Plymouth
City Council]*

House (Fig 111). Winston Churchill, suspicious of trades union control of vital
industries, did not visit until September 1941 and only long afterwards, in 1953,
was Coventry given the status of a 'lord' mayor in recognition of its resilience
and contribution to the war effort.[113] Lord Reith based his wartime policy of
'planning boldly' on Coventry and singled out Coventry with Bristol and

Birmingham for the special studies which led to the 1944 Town & Country Planning Act. It was Coventry that most influenced the zoning and road planning of the MTCP's *The Redevelopment of Central Areas*. Gibson's 1941 plan for the city centre was widely published in the home architectural press, perhaps more as an act of propaganda than in expectation of becoming reality, and articles appeared in Cuba, Argentina and America. As the revised plans emerged through the 1940s, they were published throughout Europe, America and the Soviet Union as well as in the *Architectural Review* and *Architectural Design*, the two British journals with an international distribution. *Architectural Design* devoted its December 1958 edition to Coventry (*see* p 116) and, in 1956, the Arts Council's exhibition of contemporary British building from 1945 to 1955 featured Ling's revised plans for the city centre as well as Spence's cathedral and his church at Tile Hill. Coventry was the only provincial local authority to have its buildings consistently published in the architectural and engineering press throughout the period. Uniquely too, the individual architects concerned were credited, a mark of Gibson and Ling's recognition of the contribution of the many talents in their departments.

Except for major buildings like the Cathedral, the press was largely uncritical, publication alone identifying the buildings as exemplars. Gibson, Ling and Gregory's status as architect-planners put them almost beyond criticism. Similarly, Coventry buildings were included in the *Housing Manuals* and other governmental handbooks of good practice, such as the MHLG and Ministry of Transport's 1963 *Town Centres: Current Practice* which illustrated the shopping precincts, City Market, civic centre, Hillman House and Ling's city centre plan. Some 3,500 copies of Coventry's road systems surveys, 'Shopping in Coventry', 'Work in Coventry' and 'Coventry City Region' which made up the revised Development Plan were sold or given to local authorities across the country between 1963 and 1967.[114] The accolades followed – Wellington Gardens, Tile Hill, Willenhall Wood Phase 1, Riley Square, the Belgrave Estate and Henley Road all won national architectural awards; the City Arcade and Lanchester College both won awards from the Civic Trust. Nationally and internationally, Coventry was synonymous with progressive planning and architectural ideas drawing visitors from across the globe:

> Here [the Upper Precinct], frequently, of a weekday, when the throng is no more than a scatter, you may see a knot of dark-suited, or dark-complexioned men, a delegation from abroad, guests of the city or of the British Council, inspecting Coventry's *chef d'oeuvre*, before proceeding to admire the celebrated drum-shaped market with its pioneer car-park lid: or, perhaps, less formal, the nodding, chatting planning-committee of some northern borough, eager to learn, proudly shepherded by an alderman or the city's Public Relations Officer, their next stop Tile Hill.[115]

At the same time, there was clear awareness amongst Ling and Gibson's staff of comparable developments in other places including Rotterdam and Stockholm, so that Coventry was both an influence for and was influenced by contemporary development. Nowhere was this influence clearer than in the

New Towns – Stevenage, Crawley and Harlow – being built in the early 1950s contemporary with Tile Hill, Willenhall and Wood End. The basis of their planning in distinct neighbourhood units was very similar, as were their neighbourhood centres, although their overall populations were very much smaller. Their town centres, built in the late 1950s, were all pedestrianised precincts and, without the precedent of Coventry, it is very likely that they would have followed the conventional street-access layouts shown in *The Redevelopment of Central Areas*. The centre of Stevenage, where Brian Bunch, at Coventry in 1939 and from 1945 to 1957, was deputy chief architect, was set out on a rectilinear grid surrounded by a ring road with roundabouts at grade, very similar to Gibson's initial plans for Coventry (Fig 112). Sir Frederic Osborn noted that 'a foreign architect has remarked that if you have seen Coventry and Stevenage you have seen the best contribution to urban planning that England has made since the war'.[116]

Figure 112
Stevenage town centre (L G Vincent, architect,
Stevenage Development Corporation, completed 1959).
[MHLG and MoT 1963, Plate 2]

Coventry Cathedral

Two further interconnected themes predominate in the formation of Coventry's
international reputation. The first was the expression of solidarity through
connection and, later, 'twinning' with similarly war-affected cities. Coventry's
first contact was with Stalingrad (now Volgograd) in 1942 leading to the first
ever city twinning in 1944. Visits by delegations of city councillors to Lidice,
Czechoslovakia in 1947, Belgrade, Yugoslavia in 1952 and Dresden, German
Democratic Republic in 1956 further strengthened connections. Evidence of the
links is shown in locations throughout the city from the Belgrade Theatre,
Volgograd Place, Lidice Place, Galatzi Place and Meschede Way. Twinning linked
to the second theme, that of peace and reconciliation. This was enthusiastically
taken up after the war was over, but initiated by the Provost of Coventry
Cathedral, Richard Howard, standing amongst the ruins of the bombed
cathedral only weeks after the German raid that destroyed it and declaring:

> What we want to tell the world is this, that with Christ born again in our
> hearts today, we are trying, hard as it may be, to banish all thoughts of
> revenge. We are bracing ourselves to finish this tremendous job of saving
> the world from tyranny and cruelty. We are going to try and make a
> kinder, simpler, a more Christ-child like sort of world in the days beyond
> this strife.[117]

The case of Dresden in particular merged the efforts of the City and the
Cathedral through continuing exchanges, including youth work-camps engaged
in rebuilding, to establish peace and reconciliation as a fundamental tenet of
the new Coventry.

Central to this idea was the rebuilding of the cathedral.[118] Giles Gilbert
Scott's 1944 Gothic design pleased nobody, caught between the ideas of more
progressive clergy like Howard and Bishop Gorton who thought the building
should symbolise resurrection, a conservative reconstruction committee initially
chaired by the retired Ernest Ford and those that either wanted the ruins left as a
memorial or rebuilt entirely. Although the City supported a new building, it was
nervous of government funds being diverted from other city projects and the
shortage of local building labour being exacerbated by another major project.

Also there were those, like Gibson and other younger architects, who thought that the cathedral, like the city, should be modern. The answer was the open competition held in 1951 and Basil Spence's winning design cleverly steered its way through the controversies. Essentially his cathedral was stripped Gothic with the altar conventionally beyond the choir, similar to Guildford Cathedral, designed by Edward Maufe, one of the judges. The nave ran north–south at a right angle to the old cathedral with a porch and glazed front uniting the two and picking up Gibson's axis to Broadgate. The ruins remained as an open-air memorial, the medieval spire as the only vertical element in an otherwise long, low shape sloping down towards Pool Meadow (Fig 113). But it was modern

Figure 113
Coventry Cathedral, east elevation to Priory Street with the new porch and Lady Chapel of the old cathedral (Basil Spence & Partners, 1951–62). Jacob Epstein's bronze of St Michael and the Devil on the wall of the baptistery.
[DP164703]

too, with the Chapels of Unity and Guild Chapel (Christ the Servant) expressed as separate circular forms clad in abstract fins, the aisle defined by splayed walls holding full height, gridded windows and the vast baptistery window bending out to the east. Gibson advised Hodgkinson that the cathedral 'is fine ... the design is different, it is not off the peg, it satisfies on all counts, it reveals a lot of divine inspiration and it will outlast critics'.[119]

Spence dedicated the next ten years of his career to the development and realisation of the cathedral. According to Hodgkinson, Spence 'could sell ice-cream to Eskimos' and he proved to be brilliant at dealing with the ever-changing brief, ever-changing committee (Gorton died in 1955 and Howard retired in 1958) and even, in adversity, with the diminishing budget. With the engineer Ove Arup, he developed the nave vaults, possibly the feeblest element of the competition design, into a facetted set of shallow arches clad in timber and set on impossibly thin concrete columns (Fig 114), raised the height of the porch to match the nave and greatly simplified the north end. Throughout the process he maintained the original concept and with the collaboration of the best artists of the day – including John Piper and Patrick Reyntiens, Geoffrey Clarke, Ralph Beyer, Graham Sutherland, John Hutton and Elisabeth Frink – produced a carefully choreographed, idiosyncratic and sumptuous modern interior. When it was consecrated in 1962, the finished building divided the critics. Older critics like Nikolaus Pevsner and Lewis Mumford (shown round the building by Spence himself) were generally in favour; others criticised it for what it was not – neither a true Gothic design nor a centralised church like the Catholic cathedral at Liverpool, then being constructed. A younger generation, especially the *Architectural Review*'s Reyner Banham, regarded it as an anachronism, criticising it for its concealed structure, the 'dishonesty' of its applied decoration and profusion of forms and finishes. Certainly its materials – sandstone, Westmorland slate, copper roofing, marble flooring – and integration of applied art were more in tune with the architecture of Gibson's generation than with Ling's, but the Cathedral struck a popular chord with the public. Spence's account of the building, *Phoenix at Coventry*, published in 1962, became a best seller. The Cathedral received 2½ million visitors in its first year, 60,000 visitors per year through the 1960s, rising to over 400,000 per year in the mid-1980s. It was listed Grade 1 in 1988 and in 1999 a Channel 4 and English Heritage poll voted the Cathedral Britain's favourite 20th-century building.

Figure 114
Coventry Cathedral, nave (Basil Spence & Partners, 1951–62). Graham Sutherland's tapestry of Christ in Glory behind the altar.
[DP082268]

The Coventry diaspora

Coventry's influence was not constrained. As with the extension of the peace and reconciliation programme through twinning and exchange visits, and the two-way influence of the city's reconstruction, architects and planners who passed through the City's Planning and Architecture Department were influential in other authorities at home and abroad. They took with them experience 'enriched by living with good planning on the ground'.[120] Coventry-educated staff, including Gibson and Ling, were later to be important in the development of primary planning and new approaches to education at government level, in city planning including reconstruction, the design and planning of the second generation new towns, school design and, for a few, academia.

Percy Johnson-Marshall joined the Ministry of Town & Country Planning to work on the 1947 Town & Country Planning Act, later moving to the London County Council and eventually becoming professor of Town Planning at Edinburgh University. Wilfred Burns became chief planning officer at Newcastle upon Tyne where he proposed 'that the expanded and redeveloped shopping centre based on a new system of traffic free pedestrian routes should be served by underground and multi-storey car parks and be enclosed by a system of urban motorways'.[121] He became president of the Royal Town Planning Institute (1967–8) and chief planning officer to the MHLG. Fred Pooley became county architect at Buckinghamshire where he worked on ideas for what would become the new town of Milton Keynes, was president of the RIBA between 1973 and 1975 and, later, chief architect to the Greater London Council. Fred Lloyd Roche became general manager of Milton Keynes Development Corporation after working on Runcorn new town with Ling. Brian (Bill) Berrett was Fred Pooley's personal assistant developing the ideas for North Bucks New City and moved to Milton Keynes as executive architect and then director of planning, later becoming director of planning and social development at Auckland, New Zealand and, subsequently, teaching at Leeds University. Other county architects included Raymond Ash of Surrey, Kenneth King of Norfolk and John Barker of Bedfordshire; Michael McLellan became chief architect at Waverley Borough Council in 1974 and Bill Kretchmer deputy borough architect and planning officer at the London borough of Lambeth. David Percival, deputy to both Gibson and Ling, became city architect at Norwich where London Street became one of the first pedestrianised historic streets in Britain in 1967. Brian Bunch moved from Stevenage to Redditch Development Corporation as chief architect and planner, and Don Fenter and Ceri Griffiths both worked on Telford New Town. Paul Beney was one of the Coventry architects who moved to the Metropolitan West Midlands County Planning Department where he worked on the first designs for Birmingham airport. Coventry-trained planners staffed the new planning-only departments in cities like Newcastle, Leicester and, especially, at Liverpool where Audrey Lees, Wilfred Burns's successor at Coventry, and at least four other ex-Coventry planners were appointed by the late 1960s.[122] Ray Spaxman, who 'learnt his trade' under Douglas Beaton, became chief planning officer in Vancouver, Canada where the concepts of 'Vancouverism' resonated with aspects of Coventry.[123]

No other local authority office, except for the very much larger London County Council, could boast of such influence. As Hodgkinson recalled:

> Coventry had been fortunately blessed with teams of young and enthusiastic architects and planners. An architect of international fame once said 'Divine guidance led the City Fathers to choose Donald Gibson and Arthur Ling' but he did not venture an opinion as to the sort of guidance given them in other respects, nor that but for the sanctions given by the Labour City Council, none of their bright ideas could have got off the ground. My own opinion is that there has been a single-mindedness at least about the fundamentals which have faced the technical and professional staff at all levels.[124]

8

Coventry after 1973

The 1970s and 1980s were not kind to Coventry. In the space of a few years the motor and engineering industries, on which Coventry's wealth depended, collapsed. The continued financial and physical growth that had been assumed since the war faltered and stopped; in the early 1980s over 20 per cent of the workforce was unemployed. Standard-Triumph at Canley closed in 1980, Morris Engines at Courthouse Green in 1981 and Herbert Engineering, whose founder Sir Alfred Herbert was the benefactor of the Art Gallery and Cathedral, closed in 1983. It was particularly tough on the young, now staying on at school until aged 16, who found that there were no engineering apprenticeships. It was also disillusioning for the older generation, like George Hodgkinson, who found the city 'informed with values which had no place in his concept of what a city should be'.[125] With less money to spend, a city centre devoted only to shopping became deserted, the *Ghost Town* of the Specials song of 1981. The Locarno closed to be converted into the City Library only because the space was available and there was no money or the political will to complete the original grand project next to the Herbert.[126] In an attempt to revive the empty shops, a ramped access from Broadgate (1979–81) incorporating a kiosk was built to the upper level and the walkway converted to a wide semicircular form, but it blocked Gibson's axis and views of the cathedral spire and the new undercroft must have been dark and gloomy.

By this time the city architect and planning officer was Harry Noble (b 1934), appointed in 1973 to replace Gregory who had become the first chief executive of the new metropolitan district council of Coventry, reorganised under the Local Government Act of 1972. Noble was a graduate of the architecture department of Huddersfield School of Art and planning department of Leeds University and had been assistant chief architect at Birmingham from 1967. Under the Act, strategic planning was transferred to a new West Midlands regional authority, taking staff from Coventry, and part of Noble's job was to slim down a department with less work in a city in economic decline. Increasingly his job became one of economic development rather than design, and in 1986 his title was changed to Director of Economic Development and Planning. Noble found a city still under the shadow of Gibson and unprepared for change, noting that 'Gibson, Ling and Gregory made omelettes, and I picked up the shells'.[127] He identified the need for Coventry to adjust from an engineering to a service based economy, establishing the Science Park and

Phoenix Initiative: Glass bridge and spiral ramps, Millennium Place (MacCormac Jamieson Prichard, architects, with Whitby Bird, engineers, and Alex Beleschenko, artist, and Speirs and Major, lighting designers, 1997–2003).
[© Marc Goodwin, Archmospheres; www.archmospheres.com]

Business Park adjacent to Warwick University, and created the first areas of specifically middle-class housing in the south of the city at Westwood and off Gibbet Hill Road. Noble retired in 1994 and the post of city architect and planning officer was not revived.

The suburbs after 1973

In the suburbs, with rising prices and rising rates, the cost of heating the 'no-fines' houses, especially in the poorer areas such as Wood End and Willenhall and in the flats of Hillfields, became prohibitive. In 1974, a damning report from Shelter, the national campaign for the homeless, revealed that houses and flats, some of them barely 15 years old, were suffering from chronic damp and condensation, making them uninhabitable.[128] Furthermore there were complaints of accumulating rubbish, inadequate repairs and insensitive management from the City, also strapped for cash and unused to such problems on such a scale. Worst affected was Wood End, at the greatest distance from the city centre, where almost half the population was under 15, a quarter of the tenants had rent arrears and community facilities were the least adequate. Vandalism was rife and over 20 percent of the tenants were on a transfer list to move to other estates, destroying any possibility of a cohesive community. The tenants blamed the City, the City blamed the tenants and some blamed the architecture for its technical inadequacies and layouts, especially the small gardens, common front greens and lack of privacy. There were no quick fixes for such problems, which were not unique to Coventry. The 'right to buy' of the 1980s shifted responsibility to owners (although, later, it fuelled 'buy to let') but better management and, eventually, economic recovery gradually improved the appearance of the estates and the ever-changing sociological issues were, perhaps, better understood. However, in May 1992, with male unemployment in Wood End at 49 per cent, there were riots lasting ten days and spreading to Willenhall and Hillfields.

In 2000, the City transferred its stock of 22,000 houses to Whitefriars Housing Association, the largest single such transfer in the country. Most of the ten-storey blocks at Hillfields were demolished and, since 2010 under the 'Spirit Quarters' initiative, major demolitions have commenced at Wood End (Fig 115).

Figure 115
Wimpey 'no fines' houses, Bretford Road, Wood End
awaiting demolition in 2013.
[© the authors]

The rows of 'no-fines' terraces have been replaced with brick houses resembling the standard types produced by speculative developers, avoiding any innovative layouts but increasing the density and decreasing the size of gardens. Elsewhere, the majority of the houses and flats of the post-war estates remain in original, if shabby, condition, altered only by the ubiquitous white plastic windows and occasional added pitched roofs. Even the Stonebridge Highway estate and the BISF houses at Canley are still there. The paintings of the artist George Shaw, shortlisted for the Turner Prize in 2011, depict his Tile Hill scarred by time but somehow defiant and idyllic (Fig 116). Whereas most local authorities have demolished their 1960s tower blocks, in Coventry they remain, and when refurbished, for example at William Batchelor House, Thomas King House and Alpha House (which *celebrated* its 50th anniversary in 2013), continue to provide wonderful small flats with a view. The refurbishments have greatly improved the immediate landscapes around the towers and the security of the entrances. The equivalent spaces in the housing estates have hardly changed at all – they are still the original open, 'social democratic' landscapes criticised by Shelter in 1974 and the residents of Woodway Lane in 1967. Only the garage courtyards have changed, usually by removing the garages to deter vandalism and to provide more parking spaces.

Figure 116 (left)
'This Sporting Life' by George Shaw, 2009. Humrol enamel on board. Houses off Dunhill Avenue, Tile Hill viewed from the recreation ground (known locally as 'The Poderosa') on Broad Lane.
[Courtesy of the Wilkinson Gallery, London (Private Collection); © George Shaw]

Figure 117 (opposite, above)
Cathedral Lanes Shopping Centre, Broadgate (Chapman Taylor & Partners, 1985–9). Lady Godiva turned to face down the axis of the Upper Precinct.
[DP164612]

New shopping in the city centre

The 1980s reversed the old order of local authority control and initiative. Development now relied upon private speculators and private money alone and the City, desperate for new investment, was unable to resist the commercial imperative. The Cathedral Lanes Shopping Centre (1985–9 by Chapman Taylor & Partners of London; Fig 117), a developer-led competition and the first new shops since Hertford Street, replaced Gibson's temporary shops facing Broadgate and the pre-war Martin's Bank on High Street. Gibson and Ling's visions of an open space leading to the Cathedral disappeared forever to be replaced by an enclosed mall, on the fashionable American model, clothed in thin polychrome brickwork of vaguely classical origins, and fronted with a modish tent (now removed) which covered the Godiva statue. Lady Godiva was turned to face west down Broadgate, so that it was she and Chapman Taylor's faux pediment, not the cathedral spire, that now terminated Gibson's axis.

Figure 118
West Orchards Shopping Centre, Smithford Way (John Clark Associates, 1986–91).
[DP164638]

Next, the West Orchards Shopping Centre (1986–91, by John Clark Associates of London), between Smithford Way and Ironmonger Row, replaced the car park and Gibson's modest shops on Smithford Way (Fig 118). It took land from the street, reducing its width by one third and blocked the once axial view of Hillman House. It was also an American-style mall, but totally inward looking so that a large block of the city stretching through to the Upper Precinct was privatised. To make it more accessible, the developer demanded the removal of the Locarno (Library) stair to clear the remainder of Smithford Way and installed a covered escalator filling the Upper Precinct. The upper walkways were crudely redesigned and Gibson's elegant curved staircases, Walter Ritchie's sculpted panels, the pool and the cherry trees were removed by 1993.[129] Far from being the meeting and lingering space Gibson intended, the Precinct was converted to a convenient access to a shopping mall (Fig 119). Although a project to roof the Upper Precinct was abandoned, with the redevelopment of Broadgate and West Orchards, the commercial focus of the whole shopping centre moved eastwards, leaving the Lower Precinct behind. To revive it, the City entered into a partnership with a developer who proposed a glazed roof over the whole space (1994–2002, designed by Aukett Associates of London), widening the access ramp, extending the shops and removing the canopy between Woolworth's and the Library. There were discussions about conserving and listing the original design, but the scheme appeared to be an

Figure 119
Upper Precinct reordered with escalator to West
Orchards Shopping Centre (John Clark Associates,
1986–91).
[DP164623]

acceptable balance between the new and the old. Realised, however, it was an unhappy compromise: the roof was clumsy and intrusive, the polished stone paving scale-less and the poor Godiva Café, stripped of its mullions and blinds and within a weatherproof enclosure, rendered irrelevant (Fig 120). Gordon Cullen's tiled murals were partly rescued and fixed to the entrance passage from Corporation Street, still a narrow, claustrophobic space which surely should have been redesigned.

The demolition of the New Hippodrome[130] in 2002 left the Belgrade as the only theatre in the city centre. In the area west of Queen Victoria Road, zoned in 1945 for light industrial use, the old GEC factory was demolished and replaced with the Skydome Arena (1999, S & P Architects of London) consisting of a 4,200 seat multi-purpose hall, a nine-screen cinema, an ice rink and a multi-storey car park (Fig 121). The architecture was the architecture of 'tin' industrial sheds and the buildings were crammed against the ring road and surrounded by service roads with no obvious fronts or backs, except that a fake 19th-century 'factory' façade faced Spon Street in an attempt to 'blend in' with

Figure 120
Glass roof over the reordered Lower Precinct. Aukett Associates 1994-2002. The Lady Godiva Café just visible within. In the foreground the roofs of Woolworth's, left, the Locarno (City Library), right, and the tower of Mercia House beyond.
[26495_023]

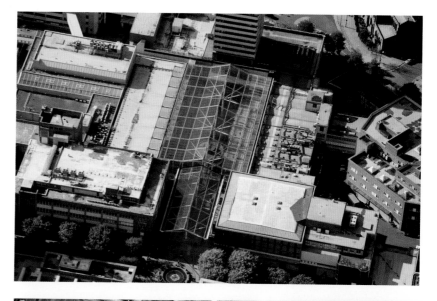

Figure 121
Coventry Skydome, Odeon Cinema and Arena (Planet Ice ice rink), between Croft Road and Spon Street; Ikea store, Queen Victoria Road (S & P Architects, 1999; Capita Ruddle Wilkinson, 2004–7). The 19th-century terraces of Starley Road, bottom right.
[26495_008]

the medieval street. Nothing in its appearance or use enhanced the complexity and grain of the area and this was compounded by the addition, on Queen Victoria Road of the seven-storey Ikea store (2004–7 by Capita Ruddle Wilkinson of Peterborough), the only such in-town store in Britain. At a new and gross scale, it dwarfed the little houses to the south and did nothing to enliven the street (Fig 122). The planning of this area is in stark contrast to the care taken for the Phoenix Initiative (1997–2003), which created a new route between the Cathedral and the Coventry Transport Museum on Hales Street through a series of squares, revealing Coventry's ancient historic fabric and terminating in a new public space, Millennium Place.[131] The plan (master planned by MacCormac Jamieson Prichard of London) included for the first time in the centre of the city, a mixture of shops, offices and flats together with a visitor centre for the priory ruins and grasped the opportunity to refurbish various old buildings, the whole unified by an inventive, small-scale landscape stretching over Millennium Place to Lady Herbert's Gardens (Fig 123 and *see* p 128).

Figure 122
Ikea store, Queen Victoria Road
(Capita Ruddle Wilkinson, 2004–7).
[DP164665]

Figure 123
Phoenix Initiative, Priory Place shops and flats
(MacCormac Jamieson Prichard, 1997–2003).
[DP164680]

The civic precinct and Coventry University

Noble completed the Sports and Recreation Centre (changing the cladding from lead to zinc) and completed the civic precinct. The corner of the Earl Street offices (1974–6)[132] took account of the pedestrian route from Little Park Street into Earl Street and the undercroft of the Architecture and Planning Department. Ling had drawn a simple square plan to connect the two existing wings and Gibson had suggested a bridge to the Council House as early as 1947. Noble's brief included a new entrance and meeting rooms and the square plan was enlarged but with chamfered corners. The ground floor entrance was recessed for a walkway enclosed by bold, slanting brick columns. The upper floor openings were recessed behind deep, angled brick reveals and the considerable mass was capped with a steep pyramidal copper roof, cousin to that of the Sports Centre (Fig 124). The bridge, also of copper, copied the angled forms in miniature, and collided with one of the stone mullioned windows of the Council House (*see* Fig 2). The greatest surprise was the brickwork – Gibson's gentle Blockley brick was replaced by bright-red Accrington engineering brick, selected for its strength and the (low) cost of the specially shaped bricks required. These were in fashion due to James Stirling's 'red' (brick) buildings at Leicester, Cambridge and Oxford and another almost contemporary example, the Divisional Fire Station (1973–5)[133] on the ring road at Radford Road, displayed similar angled forms and intense brickwork details. Otherwise, the Earl Street offices are stylistically independent, mediating successfully between Gibson's Scandinavian and Garrett & Simister's Tudor, terminating the civic gardens and punctuating the corner of Little Park Street.

The Magistrates' Court and Crown and County Court completed the southern part of the civic precinct, but not as intended by Ling, nor as by Noble who, in 1975, proposed one massive courts building.[134] Noble's Magistrates' Court (1984–7)[135] was a solid mass of red brickwork with a chamfered corner flanked by twin stair towers facing Meschede Way and the civic gardens (Fig 125). Its building line neither aligned to the Police Station nor to the Civic Offices, suggesting that the upper part of the street was to become a distinct 'place'. The separate Crown Court (1986), designed by the PSA Midland Region with the John Madin Design Group, was hidden behind and in white Portland stone with a zinc-clad pitched 'shed' roof – curious choices amongst the campus of brick and copper. Its severe rectangular form took little account of the shape or contours of its site and a portentous ramp connected it to Much Park Street.

By the 1990s, the northern part of the civic precinct might properly be relabelled the university precinct, taking in all of Ling and Gregory's buildings, altering or demolishing Ling's Miesian group, and establishing a set of new buildings east of the ring road and Much Park Street. These began modestly but, as the institution's confidence grew and it realised that sparkling new buildings were important to image and recruiting in a competitive business,

Figure 124
Civic Offices, Little Park Street and Earl Street (Harry Noble, city architect and planning officer, 1974–6).
[DP164972]

Figure 125
Magistrates' Court, Little Park Street (Harry Noble, director of economic development and planning, 1984–7).
[DP172630]

they became more extreme. Alan Short & Associates of Stamford produced the eccentric Lanchester Library (1998–2000); Arup Associates of London designed the geometric Faculty of Engineering and Computing (2008); Hawkins\Brown of London demolished the Lanchester College workshops and replaced them with the Hub (2011), the new student centre of the university with its shiny glass cladding leading to Spence's cathedral canopy (Fig 126). At the end of this, on Priory Street, the Herbert has been revived with extensions to its galleries (2004) by Haworth Tomkins of London and new History Centre (2002–8) by Pringle Richards Sharratt of London, the latter taking the form of a timber lattice arch supposedly inspired by Spence's nave vault (Fig 127). Despite the quality of the recent buildings, the university precinct has yet to achieve the cohesiveness that Gibson, Ling and Gregory intended for their city.

Figure 126 (above)
The Hub, Coventry University (Hawkins\Brown, 2011). The cathedral spire beyond Priory Street in the distance.
[DP164701]

Figure 127 (left)
History Centre, Herbert Art Gallery and Museum, Priory Street (Pringle Richards Sharratt, 2002–8).
[DP164708]

Conservation and opportunity

The pioneering ideas that defined the 'socialist city' – the car-free pedestrianised precincts, the public ownership of spaces, the greens, the parks and woodlands, the Radburn housing, the communal neighbourhood centres, the prefabricated schools – seem very distant from modern Coventry. A few of the buildings from this period are regarded as 'historic' and are listed by the Secretary of State for Culture, Media and Sport as buildings of special architectural or historic interest, demonstrating 'that the best of modern architecture ranks with that of the past, and will equally stand the test of time'.[136] In the city centre, these are Broadgate House, Coventry Cathedral, Belgrade Theatre, City Market, Railway Station and the Central Swimming Baths, the Godiva statue in Broadgate and Mitchell's mural sculptures on the Three Tuns. In the suburbs, only Christchurch, Cheylesmore and Spence's three little churches, Woodlands School and Limbrick Woods Junior and Infants schools are listed.[137] Indeed the major change to the suburbs has been the demolition and rebuilding of Coventry's post-war schools. The steel and aluminium building systems did not fail but from 1997 central government made funding available for replacement rather than repair and refurbishment and, of course, the new schools were more efficient in terms of staffing, resources and energy use. The City authorities and head teachers could only acquiesce and arguments for conservation fell on deaf ears. Just as the city threw away its unique medieval timber heritage, it is likely that those few post-war schools still remaining will soon be demolished. A great era of British architecture will have been erased. Perhaps there is now, among the residents, a tacit understanding of the special nature of the suburbs but that has yet to be expressed in terms of explicit conservation by defining what principal characteristics could and should be preserved, improved or changed. The houses cannot be demolished en masse but can be upgraded to modern standards (as Whitefriars have demonstrated) but now, with diverse ownerships, it is much more difficult to agree and enact communal projects on an estate-wide scale. The danger is that ad hoc, small-scale changes and local, uncoordinated maintenance will degrade the overall quality of the historic environment, affecting all residents. The consistent architecture, gardens, local shopping and generous parkland and woodland settings are potentially a formula for genuinely sustainable communities but it is difficult to see what agencies could bring this about.

No doubt there are other buildings which should be considered for listing and this status does not inhibit well-considered additions and alterations as the smart extension to the Belgrade Theatre by Stanton Williams of London (2002–7) has proved. Significant places may be conserved as conservation areas but, like the Upper and Lower Precincts, Tile Hill and Willenhall Wood, very few have survived without alterations which jeopardise their authenticity. The constant short-term changes wrought by the retail trade in particular are at odds with the long-term stability that characterises architecturally important places. The inexorable cycle of buildings being unappreciated, lack of investment and maintenance being viewed as money wasted needs to be reversed. These buildings must be regarded as assets rather than liabilities. In the city centre, this has already been demonstrated. In 2008 a project partly sponsored by the City and designed by Jerde, architects from Venice, California, proposed the demolition of 66 acres (26.7ha) of the city centre from the Upper Precinct to Corporation Street and Queen Victoria Road including the Lower Precinct, City Market and Shelton Square. It was to be replaced by 660,000sq m of offices, flats and shopping, much of it contained in a ring of vast towers surrounding an egg-shaped library. However, it failed to capture the public imagination and developers were unable to fund a project which could not be delivered in phases and would have required the closure of the whole city centre for years. The proposals were dropped to be replaced by small-scale, piecemeal alterations which took far greater account of the existing architecture and its original intentions. Broadgate was pedestrianised and repaved, somewhat as suggested by Ling in 1958, and the pedestrian underpass was removed from Warwick Road, greatly improving the connection to Greyfriars Green.[138] It is easy to see how small-scale improvements, based on an understanding of the original plan, such as restoring the Upper Precinct by removing the escalators and ramp and opening up the arch of Broadgate House, would make for a better connected, more enjoyable sequence of spaces and restore fine buildings. The quality of the original architecture is waiting to be rediscovered.

However, with 'traditional' shopping threatened by out-of-town supermarkets, retail 'parks', e-sales and, for Coventry, the attractions of nearby Birmingham, Warwick and Leamington Spa, the idea of a shopping precinct that takes up the major area of a city must be questioned. Strict functional zoning, which was the backbone of post-war planning, is now unnecessarily restrictive,

Figure 128
Project for Friargate (Allies and Morrison, 2011).
A gridded cluster of towers up to twelve-storeys high
of offices, flats, a hotel and other commercial uses is
grouped around a new station square with a direct
pedestrian link to the enlarged Greyfriars Green.
[© Allies and Morrison]

as the lively contrasts of the Phoenix Initiative and the term-time university demonstrate. This was recognised by Ling with Hillman House, Mercia House and the Locarno, but more housing and other uses in the city centre would change its monocultural bias for the better and add permanence to the vagaries of retail lettings. With mixed uses comes demand for better access. Gibson and Ling's pedestrianised city streets are fine when full of people but getting to them via multi-storey car parks and grubby service courts was never satisfactory and permanent pedestrianisation severely restricts uses other than conventional shops. There is no reason why pedestrianised streets cannot share traffic for both servicing and access to other uses, a pattern the European historic city regards as normal. In Europe, public transport to connect the railway station and the suburbs conveniently to the centre is common, but in Coventry with the ring road, the isolated bus station and pedestrianised streets, this has never been achieved adequately. If the inner city streets became more permeable, then so should their connections to the suburbs just outside the ring road, like Hillfields, Spon End and, now, Coventry University. As Buchanan predicted, the ring road has drawn a tight collar around the city centre, using and blighting acres of valuable land and severely restricting access to the centre for vehicles, cyclists and pedestrians. With the M6 motorway, eastern bypass and Phoenix Way link in place, the necessity for an urban motorway, especially one which is so tortuous to navigate, is now debatable. Were it to be replaced by an at-grade boulevard with the level pedestrian crossings and cycle lanes Gibson intended, Coventry would be a much enhanced city. A start has been made: a project for Friargate in the area north of the Railway Station by Allies and Morrison of London (2011 and ongoing; Fig 128) has demonstrated that it is possible to remove slip roads, enlarge Greyfriars Green and greatly improve the level connection from the station to the city across the ring road.

This is not to say that Coventry needs wholesale change. On the contrary, Gibson, Ling and Gregory gave Coventry a world-famous plan in the city centre and suburbs, with some fine buildings and spaces that now have unique historical significance. What Coventry needs is sensitive, informed and imaginative planning so that change can be managed in ways that continue the life, use and enjoyment of Coventry's remarkable post-war heritage.

Notes

1 Priestley 1934, 69–70

2 *Midlands Daily Telegraph* 8 Mar 1937 quoted by Hasegawa 1992, 23

3 This is discussed by Richard Crossman, Labour MP for Coventry East (1945–70), in his introduction to Hodgkinson 1970, xv–xvi

4 Walford 2009, 133

5 Hodgkinson 1970, 129

6 Gropius 1935, 44. Gropius had lectured at the Liverpool School of Architecture in 1934 and exhibited his ideas for prefabricated and high-rise housing.

7 Johnson-Marshall 1966, 293. Staff architects: J T Pinion, K Lycett, P F Burgoyne, P T Powell.

8 Ibid, 293

9 *Zeilenbau flats*: a type developed in Germany in the late 1920s as an alternative to traditional courtyard forms consisting of long, narrow blocks usually set in parallel rows intended to get light and ventilation from both sides.

10 Mumford 1938,143–222, 402–93, 489

11 Hodgkinson 1970, 168

12 Gibson 1940, 41. Lecture given to Royal Society of Arts, 4 Dec

13 Reith 1949, 424

14 The planning team in the department were J A Miller, R P King, H J Lake, B Raynor, D S Craig, W H Hulley, Percy Johnson-Marshall and T F Howe.

15 Tubbs 1942, back endpaper

16 Description from captions to plans published in Corporation of Coventry 1945 *The Future Coventry*, 36

17 Corporation of Coventry 1945, 40

18 AASTA was a national organisation but the local branch consisted mainly of staff from Gibson's department. Among other activities, it fought for equal status and pay for local authority architects and technicians compared to the private sector.

19 This figure is given by Hodgkinson 1970, 170. Hasegawa 1992, 45 gives 57,500, that is, one in four of the city's entire population.

20 Brian Bunch and Guy Oddie, assistants. The stone was paid for by John Siddeley, 1st Baron Kenilworth, former chairman of Armstrong Siddeley, and also commemorates the birth of the actress Dame Ellen Terry in 1847 in a house which stood nearby. The stone and its surround have been repositioned many times.

21 The City Standard, erected in March 1948, was donated by British Pressed Panels Ltd to display local skills in sheet metal construction.

22 Brian Bunch, chief assistant architect (development stage); Raymond Ash, chief assistant architect; Frank Moate, assistant in charge of project.

23 Coventry's contribution to the Festival of Britain is described in Gill 2001,156–60.

24 Gordon Hammond, senior architect; Paul Beney, assistant architect, for the Link Blocks and Hotel Leofric.

25 Ritchie's studio was in Kenilworth. Paul Beney, architect in Ling's department, was a model for a hand on one of the panels. The full titles of the panels are 'Man struggling to control the forces inside himself' and 'Man struggling to control the forces outside himself'. The panels were commissioned in 1954 and erected between 1957 and 1959.

26 Beazley 1962, 65 (caption to photo 5)

27 Hewitt 1966, 11

28 B Berrett, pers comm 19 August 2013

29 Figures from Coventry City Council 1961, 4

30 Ling 1958, 498 and 500

31 Douglas Beaton, principal architect; K E Bradley, W M Armstrong, R J Edwards, H W Pearson, group architects; R Deeming.

32 Ling 1958, 478 and 498

33 Michael McLellan, project architect

34 Michael McLellan, principal architect central area; Rex Chell, assistant principal architect; Paul Beney, project architect; R J Edwards, assistant principal in charge of contract; P Jackman

35 Bill Pearson, assistant architect; T R Hindley. The Lower Precinct was designed by Bill Pearson, G Youett and Jean Hanney.

36 Beazley 1962, 66

37 The hotel project designed by Carl Fisher & Associates is illustrated in *The Builder* 6 July 1962, 18

38 Frank Barnett, senior architect central area

39 Michael McLellan, principal architect central area; Paul Beney, project architect

40 Hewitt 1966, 11

41 Douglas Beaton, principal architect; Kenneth Bradley, senior group architect; Ralph Iredale, assistant architect; Ian Crawford, junior assistant architect; I P Rennie, A D Newall, R I Spaxman, M McLellan, S B Downs, G J Bryson. The roundabout was designed by David Mason.

42 Ralph Iredale, assistant architect; Ian Crawford, junior assistant architect. Figures of mermaids, sailors and Neptune which adorned the cast-iron columns were by James Brown of Ling's department. These are now relocated in the City Market.

43 Lewison and Billingham 1969, 41

44 Kenneth King, group architect; Douglas Beaton, principal architect; H W Pearson, K Edgar, Michael McLellan, W M Armstrong, Jean Hanney, G J Bryson, assistant architects. Later, Paul Beney redesigned the coffee bar.

45 The aims of the 'Theatre in Education' project started in 1964 by Anthony Richardson, the second director of the Belgrade, involving schools and young people in Coventry.

46 Wesker's plays *Chicken Soup with Barley* (1958) and *Roots* (1959) premiered at the Belgrade, as did Turner's *Semi-Detached* (1962), for which Ling designed the sets (information from Brian Berrett). Berrett recalls that the boxes in the auditorium 'caused some fluttering in such an egalitarian design team'.

47 Architects for the square and Newsam's showroom were Michael McLellan, principal architect central area and Paul Beney, project architect.

48 The Kharkov theatre form recurs in Breuer & Yorke's project for a 'Civic Centre of the Future' designed for the Cement & Concrete Association in 1936. The tapered auditorium form was used in the model for the civic buildings in the Gibson's *Coventry of Tomorrow* exhibition.

49 W George Sealey, principal architect; William G Mann, project architect; M H J Robertson, J W Knight, assistant architects

50 Ling 1958, 500. A city plan showing the proposed towers accompanied the article.

51 The first designs for the south and west wings of the civic offices were published in *Building* January 1951, 14–15.

52 W George Sealey, principal architect; W Houghton-Evans, group architect in succession to H John Humby; Brian (Bill) Berrett, assistant architect; L O Davies. The mural in the reception lobby was by Michael McLellan.

53 The two institutions combined to become Lanchester Polytechnic in 1970, changing to Coventry Polytechnic in 1987 and Coventry University in 1992.

54 Michael McLellan, principal architect central area division; Paul Beney, assistant in charge; K King, E Holt and Mary E Woods.

55 Lewison and Billingham 1969, 55

56 W George Sealey, chief assistant architect (1950); John C Barker, principal assistant architect (1950); William (Bill) Kretchmer, schools architect (1958); R Grainger, group leader (1958); Michael J Bench, job architect (1958); F E Thomas, J S Smith.

57 The four college buildings were designed under Fred Lloyd Roche, assistant principal architect; David White, assistant architect, was the designer of the building.

58 Terry Long, assistant principal architect

59 The barracks is described in Glendinning 2012, 196–211.

60 Coventry City Council 1961, 47

61 Dame Evelyn Sharp at RIBA Symposium 'High Flats' February 1955 quoted by Gold 2007, 171

62 Gwyn Morris, principal architect housing; Ceri Griffiths, job architect

63 Ling 1958, 501

64 Lewison and Billingham 1969, 60

65 Ling 1958 , 501

66 Gwyn Morris, principal architect housing; in association with H Stanley Smith, chief architect of Costain, and Granville Berry, city engineer and surveyor

67 See Long 1986, 265. Coventry was a pioneer in the use of computers, installing their first IBM 626 for wages records by April 1954.

68 Buchanan 1963, 172–3

69 Long 1986, 298

70 G R Stone was a former employee of the City Architect's Department. The original elevations of the De Vere were rejected by the Planning Department and redesigned by Michael McLellan.

71 Terry Long succeeded by K L Blackburn, assistant principal architect; J D Murray, job architect

72 Michael McLellan, principal architect central area (to 1974); Granville Lewis and David Humphris, project architects

73 John Smith, principal architect

74 Michael McLellan, principal architect central area; Brian Willmott, assistant architect

75 Brian (Bill) Berrett, assistant architect, succeeded by Rex Chell, assistant principal architect

76 Described in 'Coventry Point: Market Way, Coventry' in Architecture West Midlands 28, December 1976, 43–4. The partner in charge was Derek Davis, job architect Douglas Hickman. City planning policy in 1968 defined areas of 'concentrated brightness and advertising' to promote 'interest and variety' according to Gregory 1973, 117

77 See Richardson 1972, 305

78 The adjacent northlit factory was the home of the Architecture and Planning Department before it moved to Earl Street. The factory was demolished to make way for Bull Yard.

79 Michael McLellan, principal architect central area; Rex Chell, assistant principal architect; T C Ward, assistant architect

80 Nairn 1968, 470 quoted by Gill 2004, 59–86. This is a full account of the complex history of Spon Street.

81 Initially the architects were J A Miller, R P King, H J Lake, R B Raynor, D S Craig, W H Hulley, Percy Johnson-Marshall and T E Howe and, by 1942, Gwyn H Morris, senior assistant; Betty Benson and J Thompson, assistant architects.

82 To comply with Air Raid Precautions (ARP) requirements according to *Architects' Journal* 1941, 273–6. The project was curtailed due to wartime restrictions in 1941. The houses had precast concrete stairs, concrete floors and perforated concrete entrance canopies. Gibson's initial, unbuilt design for Canley was based on F W B & F R S Yorke's housing for Flower's Brewery at Stratford-upon-Avon (1938–9), brick terraces with oversailing mono-pitch roofs.

83 The GBS house was sponsored by Gyproc Products, Brockhouse and Joseph Sankey & Sons Ltd, *see Architect & Building News* 1944, 122–5. It was on a 4ft (1.2m) grid plan with 4ft x 2ft (1.2 x 0.6m) asbestos cement cladding panels and a flat roof.

84 'No fines' concrete made from cement and coarse aggregate without fine sand and poured between standardised shuttering up to four storeys high. The system did not require skilled labour on site and the walls for a two-storey house could be ready in 24 hours. The rough concrete was rendered externally and plastered internally and traditional tiled pitched roofs were added.

85 For an account of the Stonebridge Highway estate *see* Walford 2009, 219–27

86 The *Housing Manual* and details of the 1944 Dudley Report which led to it are described in Bullock 2002 154–65. The 1949 revision reduced the recommended floor areas.

87 Councillor J C Lee Gordon *Coventry Standard* 31 August 1946 quoted in Kynaston 2007, 158

88 Sharp 1946, 60 and 63

89 Ibid, 60

90 Edmond C Tory, principal assistant architect; George Grey, chief assistant architect

91 Pevsner and Wedgwood 1966, 281

92 Gwyn Morris, principal architect housing; Matt Wallace, D Lyddon and C Griffiths, job architects. Matt Wallace was the major designer of the estate.

93 Barstable, Basildon designed by Anthony B Davis, architect to Basildon Development Corporation, and Vange 7, Basildon (1955–9) designed by Basil Spence were partially Radburn layouts. Radburn Close, Tye Green, Harlow (*c* 1955–62) designed by Frederick Gibberd is also partially Radburn, but the houses face the access roads.

94 Information from a rare tenant survey in *Official Architecture and Planning* December 1967, 1746–65

95 Gwyn Morris, principal architect housing

96 Paul Beney, project architect; the flats designed by Rex Chell. The scheme won an RIBA Regional Award in 1971.

97 Designed by Rex Chell, project architect

98 Burns 1959, 27–48. *See also* Burns 1954, 128–48

99 D E Percival, deputy city architect and planning officer; Edmond C Tory and H W Pearson, assistant architects

100 Gwyn Morris succeeded by Alan Robinson, principal architects housing; Stanley Sellars, assistant architect

101 Lewison and Billingham 1969, 129

102 From 1957 to 1958 spending in Coventry on libraries had been 10.6 (old) pence per head, less than any other town with a population of more than 100,000 and less than the Government's recommendation of 24 pence. From 1966 to 1957 Coventry spent £122 per thousand population on new books, the lowest but one for the county boroughs which averaged £172 per thousand. In 1970, stock and books on loan were the lowest of any county borough. Information from Richardson 1972, 271

103 *Architects' Journal* 20 Mar 1958, 423

104 The other N F Cachemaille-Day churches are St George, Barkers' Butts Lane, Coundon; St Luke, Rotherham Road, Holbrooks and Holy Cross, St Austell Road, Caludon all built *c* 1939.

105 Arnold Hartley Gibson, an hydraulic engineer, was professor of Engineering at Manchester University from 1920.

106 Almost contemporary schools are William Glare's Parkgate Primary School, Whitmore Park (*c* 1950) and St Christopher's Primary School, Allesley (1950–4) with similar linear plan forms.

107 Information on Coventry schools from Saint 1987 which remains the standard work on post-war schools.

108 A second smaller school, Aldermoor Farm Primary, Whitworth Avenue, Stoke Aldermoor was built using BAC MkIA system before 1955.

109 W A James, architect-in-charge; Michael J Bench, D J Chalk, J M Vauser, assistant architects

110 Richardson 1972, 214-242 and Tiratsoo 1990, 119–24

111 Council houses were also sold in Bristol and Brighton. *See* Jones 2010, 510–39

112 *See* Gould 2010

113 This is discussed in Smith 2006, 142–62. The first Lord Mayor was Alderman H B W Cresswell in 1953.

114 *See* Long 1986, 322–5

115 Hewitt 1966, 11

116 Osborn 1963, 161. The architect is not named.

117 Provost Richard Howard, broadcast from the cathedral ruins, Christmas Day 1940, recording at the Herbert Art Gallery and Museum, Coventry.

118 The complex story of the Cathedral is definitively told in Campbell 1996.

119 Quoted by Hodgkinson 1970, 201 on the occasion of the announcement of the competition results.

120 Hodgkinson 1970, 172

121 Burns 1963, 211, written in 1961

122 Long 1986, 321

123 R Spaxman, pers comm 9 July 2013

124 Hodgkinson 1970, 172. The 'architect of international fame' is not named.

125 George Hodginson quoted in Seabrook 1978, 172

126 The first stage of the Central Library (1965–7) adjoined the Herbert Art Gallery and Museum facing Bayley Lane. Michael McLellan, principal architect central area; Rex Chell succeeded by Paul Beney, project architects. The building was demolished for the History Centre.

127 H Noble, pers comm 12 Sept 2013

128 Coventry Community Workshop et al *c* 1974

129 Walter Ritchie's panels were removed in June 1993 and re-erected on the south wall of the Herbert Art Gallery and Museum in February 1994.

130 The New Hippodrome had become the Coventry Theatre in 1955, the Coventry Apollo in 1979 and, finally, Granada Bingo in 1985. It closed in 2000.

131 The full story of the Phoenix Initiative is told in McGuigan et al 2004. Millennium Place is the site of the New Hippodrome and the project also removed Gregory's car park and shops on Fairfax Street (1969). The Transport Museum opened in 1980 in the buildings of the ironfounders, Matterson Huxley & Watson, on Cook Street. The new entrance building was added on Millennium Place in 2004.

132 Rex Chell, job architect, succeeded by Roger Arlidge

133 Alan Robinson, project architect, succeeded by N Love

134 Paul Beney, project architect; Michael Tastard, assistant architect

135 Roger Arlidge, architect in charge

136 Howarth, Alan, Minister for the Arts, in the Forward to Harwood 2003

137 All are listed at Grade II except for the Godiva statue at Grade II* and Coventry Cathedral at Grade I.

138 Designed by Jacobs Babtie with Coventry City Council Design and Landscape Team.

References and further reading

Abercrombie, P and Brueton, B F 1930 *Bristol and Bath Regional Planning Scheme*. Liverpool: University Press of Liverpool Ltd and Hodder & Stoughton

Abercrombie, P 1943 *Town and Country Planning*, 2 edn. London, New York, Toronto: Oxford University Press

Abercrombie, P and Forshaw, J H 1943 *County of London Plan*. London: Macmillan

Abercrombie, P and Paton Watson, J 1943 *A Plan for Plymouth*. Plymouth: Underhill

Alker Tripp, H 1942 *Town Planning and Road Traffic*. London: Edward Arnold

Beazley, E 1962 'Coventry'. *Architects' Journal* 11 July

Bournville Trust 1941 *When We Build Again*. London: George Allen & Unwin

Buchanan, C 1963 *Traffic in Towns: A Study of the Long Term Problems of Traffic in Urban Areas*. London: HMSO

Bullock, N 2002 *Building the Post-War World: Modern Architecture and Reconstruction in Britain*. London: Routledge

Burns, W 1954 'The Coventry sociological survey: Results and interpretation'. *Town Planning Review* July

Burns, W 1959 *British Shopping Centres*. London: Leonard Hill

Burns, W 1963 *New Towns for Old*. London: Leonard Hill

Campbell, L 1996 *Coventry Cathedral: Art and Architecture in Post-War Britain*. Oxford: Clarendon

Corporation of Coventry 1945 *The Future Coventry*. Coventry: Coventry Corporation Public Relations Department

Coventry City Council 1961 *Development and Redevelopment in Coventry*. Coventry: Coventry Corporation Public Relations Department

Coventry Community Workshop, Ormandy, D and Hodge, H c 1974 *Coventry Council Houses: The New Slums*. London: Shelter

Cullen, G 1961 *Townscape*. London: The Architectural Press (reprinting articles first published in the *Architectural Review* through the 1950s)

Demidowicz, G 2003 *A Guide to the Buildings of Coventry*. Stroud: Tempus

Gibson, D 1940 'Problems of reconstruction'. *Architect & Building News* 6 Dec

Gibson, D, Barratt, C and Marshall, A H 1952 *Coventry Development Plan 1951*. Coventry: Coventry City Council

Gill, R 2001 'Restive rather than festive: Coventry and the Festival of Britain' in *Twentieth Century Architecture 5: Festival of Britain*. London: Twentieth Century Society

Gill, R 2004 'From the Black Prince to the Silver Prince: Relocating medieval Coventry' in Harwood, E and Powers, A (eds) *Twentieth Century Architecture 7: The Heroic Period of Conservation*. London: The Twentieth Century Society

Glendinning, M 2012 'Building for the Modern Soldier: Hyde Park Cavalry Barracks' in Campbell L, Glendinning M and Thomas J (eds) *Basil Spence Buildings & Projects*. London: RIBA Publishing

Gold, J R 2007 *The Practice of Modernism: Modern Architects and Urban Transformation, 1954–1972*. Abingdon: Routledge

Gould, J 2010 *Plymouth: Vision of a Modern City*. Swindon: English Heritage

Gregory, T 1973 'Coventry' in Holliday, J (ed) *City Centre Redevelopment*. London: Charles Knight

Gropius, W 1935 *The New Architecture and the Bauhaus*. London: Faber and Faber

Harwood, E 2003 *England: A Guide to Post-war Listed Buildings*. London: Batsford

Hasegawa, J 1992 *Replanning the Blitzed City Centre: A Comparative Study of Bristol, Coventry and Southampton 1941–1950*. Buckingham: OUP

Healy, Z (ed) 2012 *Rebuilding Coventry*. DVD Lincoln: University of Lincoln School of Media/Media Archive of Central England in association with ITV Studios Global Entertainment

Hewitt, J 1966 *Coventry: The Tradition of Change and Continuity*. Coventry: Coventry Corporation Public Relations Department

Historic Coventry, www.historiccoventry.co.uk

Hodgkinson, G 1970 *Sent to Coventry*. Bletchley: Robert Maxwell

Hultén, B 1951 *Building Modern Sweden*. Harmondsworth: Penguin

Johnson-Marshall, P 1966 *Rebuilding Cities*. Edinburgh: Edinburgh University Press

Jones, B 2010 'Slum clearance, privatization and residualization: The practice and politics of council housing in mid-twentieth-century England' *in Twentieth Century British History* **21** no 4. Oxford: Oxford University Press

Kidder Smith, G E 1950 *Sweden Builds*. London: The Architectural Press in cooperation with the Swedish Institute, Stockholm

Kynaston, D 2007 *Austerity Britain*. London: Bloomsbury

Le Corbusier 1929 *City of To-morrow*. London: John Rodker

Lewison, G and Billingham, R 1969 *Coventry New Architecture: A Guide to Post-war Buildings*. Warwick: The Editors

Ling, A 1958 'Looking to the future'. *Architectural Design* December 1958

Ling, A 1958 'Coventry'. *Architectural Design* December 1958

Long, M A 1986 'The post-war planning office: Coventry's Department of Architecture and Planning 1957–66'. Unpublished PhD thesis, Univ Liverpool

McGuigan, J; MacCormac, R; Lovell, V et al 2004 *Phoenix: Architecture/Art/Regeneration*. London: Black Dog

Ministry of Health 1949 *Housing Manual 1949*. London: HMSO

Ministry of Health and Ministry of Works 1944 *Housing Manual 1944*. London: HMSO

Ministry of Housing & Local Government and Ministry of Transport 1963 *Town Centres: Current Practice*. London: HMSO

Ministry of Information 1943 *Resurgam*. London

Ministry of Town and Country Planning 1947 *The Redevelopment of Central Areas*. London: HMSO

Morris, P Sir 1961 *Homes for Today and Tomorrow*. London: HMSO

Mumford, L 1938 *The Culture of Cities*. London: Secker & Warburg

Osborn, Sir F 1963 *The New Towns: The Answer to Megalopolis*. London: Leonard Hill

Pevsner, N and Pickford, C 2016 *Buildings of England: Warwickshire*. New Haven and London: Yale University Press

Pevsner, N and Wedgwood, A 1966 *The Buildings of England: Warwickshire*. Harmondsworth: Penguin

Priestley, J B 1934 *English Journey*. London: William Heineman Ltd in association with Victor Gollancz Ltd

Reith, J C W 1949 *Into the Wind*. London: Hodder & Stoughton

Richards, J M 1940 *An Introduction to Modern Architecture*. Harmondsworth: Penguin

Richardson, K 1972 *Twentieth-Century Coventry*. London: Macmillan

Royal Institute of British Architects 1943 *Towards a New Britain: Guide Book to the Rebuilding Britain Exhibition*. Cheam: The Architectural Press

Saint, A 1987 *Towards a Social Architecture: The Role of School Building in Post-War England.* New Haven and London: Yale University Press

Seabrook, J 1978 *What Went Wrong: Working People and the Ideals of the Labour Movement.* London: Victor Gollancz

Sharp, T 1940 *Town Planning.* Harmondsworth: Penguin

Sharp, T 1946 *The Anatomy of the Village.* Harmondsworth: Penguin

Smith, A 2006 'Coda – remembering the Blitz: Coventry and Southampton over sixty years on' *in* Smith, A *The City of Coventry: A twentieth century icon.* London: I B Tauris

Somake, E and Hellberg, R 1956 *Shops and Stores Today.* London: Batsford

Spence, B 1962 *Phoenix at Coventry.* London: Geoffrey Bles

Tiratsoo, N 1990 *Reconstruction, Affluence and Labour Politics: Coventry 1945–60.* London: Routledge

Tubbs, R 1942 *Living in Cities.* Harmondsworth: Penguin

Walford, S H 2009 'Architecture in tension: an examination of the position of the architect in the private and public sectors, focussing on the training and careers of Sir Basil Spence (1907–1976) and Sir Donald Gibson (1908–1991)'. Unpublished PhD thesis, Univ Warwick

Wolfe, L 1945 *The Reilly Plan – A New Way of Life.* London: Nicholson & Watson

Informed Conservation Series

This popular Historic England series highlights the special character of some of our most important historic areas and the development pressures they are facing. There are over 30 titles in the series, some of which look at whole towns such as Bridport, Coventry and Margate or distinctive urban districts, such as the Jewellery Quarter in Birmingham and Ancoats in Manchester, while others focus on particular building types in a particular place. A few are national in scope focusing, for example, on English school buildings and garden cities.

The purpose of the series is to raise awareness in a non-specialist audience of the interest and importance of aspects of the built heritage of towns and cities undergoing rapid change or facing large-scale regeneration. A particular feature of each book is a final chapter that focuses on conservation issues, identifying good examples of the re-use of historic buildings and highlighting those assets or areas for which significant challenges remain.

As accessible distillations of more in-depth research, they also provide a useful resource for heritage professionals, tackling, as many of the books do, places and buildings types that have not previously been subjected to investigation from the historic environment perspective. As well as providing a lively and informed discussion of each subject, the books also act as advocacy documents for Historic England and its partners in promoting the management of change in the historic environment.

More information on each of the books in the series and on forthcoming titles, together with links to enable them to be ordered or downloaded is available on the Historic England website.

HistoricEngland.org.uk

Coventry city centre map

(KEY cont'd on p 156)

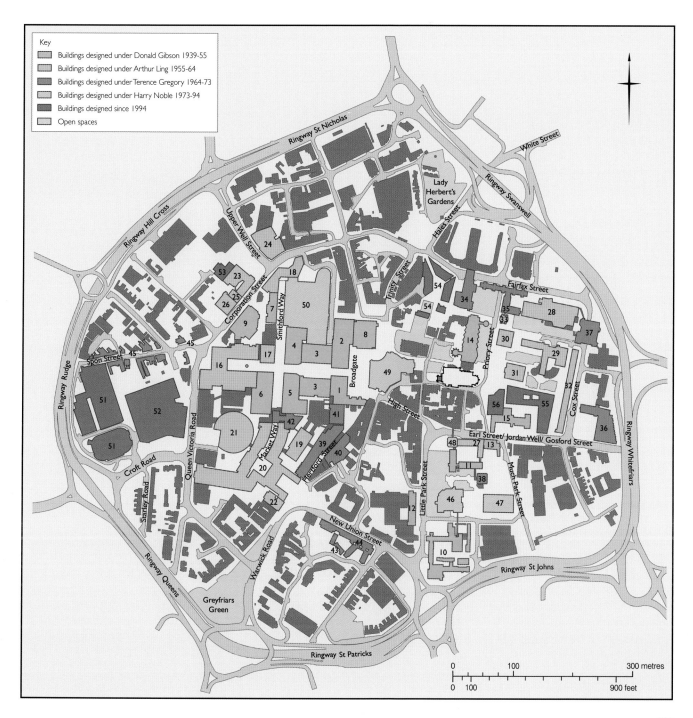

Buildings designed under Donald Gibson 1939-55

Buildings designed under Arthur Ling 1955-64

Buildings designed under Terence Gregory 1964-73

Buildings designed under Harry Noble 1973-94

Buildings designed since 1994

Open spaces

Ringway St Nicholas

White Street

Ringway Swanswell

Ringway Hill Cross

Lady Herbert's Gardens

Hales Street

Upper Well Street

Fairfax Street

Trinity Street

Corporation Street

Smithford Way

Priory Street

Spon Street

Ringway Rudge

Broadgate

High Street

Cox Street

Ringway Whitefriars

Queen Victoria Road

Market Way

Hertford Street

Little Park Street

Earl Street/ Jordan Well/ Gosford Street

Croft Road

Starley Road

Much Park Street

Warwick Road

New Union Street

Ringway St Johns

Ringway Queens

Greyfriars Green

Ringway St Patricks

0   100   300 metres

0   100   900 feet

32 Laboratory, Lanchester College (James Starley Building, Coventry University), Cox Street (CA Dept, 1957–63)

33 Hall of Residence, Lanchester College (Priory Hall, Coventry University), Priory Street (CA Dept, 1963–7)

Buildings designed under Terence Gregory 1964–73 [Coloured dark blue]

34 De Vere Hotel (Britannia Hotel), Cathedral Square, Fairfax Street (G R Stone & Associates, 1972–3)

35 Quadrant Hall (Coventry University), Fairfax Street (CA Dept, 1969–74)

36 Art College (Coventry University), Cox Street (CA Dept, 1966–7)

37 Sports and Recreation Centre, Cox Street (CA Dept, 1973–6)

38 Civic Centre tower, Little Park Street (CA Dept, 1971–3)

39 Shops and offices, Hertford Street (north-west side) (CA Dept and W S Hattrell & Partners, 1965–74)

40 Shops, Hertford Street (south-east side) (CA Dept and Redgrave & Clarke with A J Fowles & Partners, 1965–74)

41 ABC Cinema, Hertford Street (Archer Boxer & Partners, 1971–3)

42 Coventry Point, Market Way (John Madin Design Group, 1969–75)

43 Cheylesmore Manor Registry Office and extension, Manor House Drive (F W B Charles, 1966–8 and CA Dept, 1968–72)

44 Offices, New Union Street (Hellberg Harris & Partners, 1969)

45 Spon Street restorations (F W B Charles and CA Dept, 1968–75)

Buildings designed under Harry Noble 1973–94 [Coloured light blue]

46 Magistrates' Court, Little Park Street (CA Dept, 1984–7)

47 Crown Court, Much Park Street (PSA Midland Region with John Madin Design Group, 1986)

48 Civic Offices Phase 3, Earl Street (CA Dept, 1974–6)

49 Cathedral Lanes Shopping Centre, Broadgate (Chapman Taylor & Partners, 1985–9)

50 West Orchards Shopping Centre, Smithford Way (John Clark & Associates, 1986–91)

Buildings designed since 1994 [Coloured brown]

51 Skydome Arena and Ice Rink, off Croft Road (S & P Architects, 1999)

52 Ikea Store, Queen Victoria Road (Capita Ruddle Wilkinson, 2004–7)

53 Studio Theatre, Belgrade Theatre, Belgrave Square (Stanton Williams, 2002–7)

54 Phoenix Initiative and Millennium Place (MacCormac Jamieson Prichard, 1997–2003)

55 The Hub, Coventry University (Hawkins\Brown, 2011)

56 History Centre, Herbert Art Gallery and Museum, Priory Street (Pringle Richards Sharratt, 2002–8)